# Imagining the Goetheanum

*An Architectural Exploration*
*in the Language of Polar Logic*

*Jonathan Alesander*

Cover: 1919 map of the Goetheanum hill
Polar Press: ja@polarpress.org
© 2015 Jonathan Alesander
ISBN 978-0-9892628-3-5

# Contents

# The Outside

*A Walk around the Building*

*Drawing of the*
*first building motif*
*for the first*
*Goetheanum*

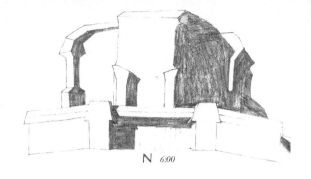

# 1

## Incarnation

Born in fire, the second Goetheanum rose from the ashes of the first Goetheanum. This incision of destruction through fire has been part of the life of many a great building. The temple to Artemis in Ephesus, considered the greatest of the seven wonders of antiquity, was destroyed by fire in 356 BC. Fulbert's great cathedral in Chartres was mostly destroyed in 1194 AD. Although phoenix-like these buildings were rebuilt, the mystery school of Ephesus and the school of Chartres, both considered the greatest centers of learning of their day, declined. In contrast, Rudolf Steiner metamorphosed the Goetheanum's architecture from the first to the second building. The first Goetheanum gave to those who came revealing its interior. The second Goetheanum awaits what human beings will bring to it, awaits for one to awaken to it in freedom.

Willed in sense material
The Goetheanum from the eternal
Speaks in forms to human eyes:
Flames could consume the material.
Let Anthroposophy
From out the spirit building
Speak to souls:
Flames of the spirit
Will temper them.

Rudolf Steiner
—from a notebook entry April 1923

### A Historical Context

The long path of the human spirit's incarnation into the physical body is witnessed in the dwellings humankind has built. At the beginnings of building, two vertical standing stones upon which a third balanced, seemingly weightless, stand as an archetype for the spirit's entry into the physical body. Megalithic cultures used a circle of such trilithons as an architectural compass for celestial direction and shadow phenomena to obtain guidance for agricultural purposes— as also with dolmens.[1] To come upon a stone circle in the wild surroundings where they are often found is a moving

experience of their enclosing, ordering principle. Equally, the earliest found remains of city-building in antiquity show the use of the grid template of intersecting straight lines for the street layout often orientated north south and east west. These laws of geometry were used to imprint their spiritual force on architecture and therewith on the human being.

The pyramids of ancient Egypt are monumental geometry. However, a great shift in building is evident in this development. Enclosed in the pyramids are internal spaces. The pyramid chambers and tombs were elaborately and exquisitely painted. However, no light shone within to illumine the wall paintings. They were not painted for the living but were dedicated to the spirit of the dead.

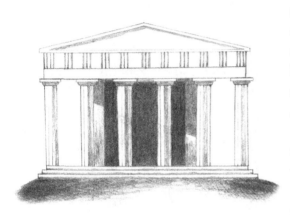

The temple architecture of ancient Greece saw the aspiration for the spirit brought into harmony with the glory of the sense world: the triangle of the spirit was raised up onto the square of the earth. The Greek temple was set in the landscape for the human eye to look up to. Its interior was not for mortals to enter but was the abode for the immortals. Alone, an oversized statue of the god stood within.

Solomon's Temple enshrined the pure abstract letter, the two tablets of the Mosaic Law. Once a year, the Holy of Holies was entered and only by the High Priest alone.

With the incarnation of the Christ, the church became a place for all to enter to consecrate the union with the god. The semidarkness, the towering vaults, the breaching perspectives, and the pinnacle of stones were fitting for prayer. Prayer was given to the Absolute in incarnation. Christ's entry into the earth was the moment of the human being's entry into the temple.

The architectural element of the columns that were placed around the Greek temple were placed inside the medieval cathedral. The column represents the verticality of the human form, the life and independent I identity. The Caryatids from the Acropolis at Athens represent maidens in a round dance with baskets of living reeds on their heads (drawing, page 6).

The exterior support for the medieval cathedral did not cease but came in a new form with the innovation of the flying buttress. To the vertical support (buttress) was added a horizontal support (flyer). The load of the roof was indirectly supported by countering the lateral loads pushing outward from the wall, which allowed for the stained glass windows with their education of the soul life. The sculptural figures in the niches of the cathedral buttresses portray the spiritual presence of angel or saint sustaining the edifice (drawings, page 6).

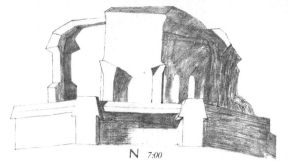

N 7:00

Medieval town-building epitomized an unconscious and deep feeling for organic, or living, building. The irregular streets and houses follow upon one another with a delight of surprise and an interest that is always embedded in harmony. Not the structure of will behind geometry, but the richness of feeling arising out of the contemplation of the Incarnation gave the impetus to build.

On this passage of the human being's incarnation into the physical body that the history of architecture expresses, the Goetheanum stands as a beginning for a new orientation in architecture. The forms of the Goetheanum bring to expression in architecture the new element of metamorphosis—as well as many other unique building elements such as the pillar forms that stand simultaneously outside (of the building's upper portion) and yet inside (of the building's lower portion). The relationship of metamorphosis in architecture frees the thinking of the human being to awaken to the spirit.

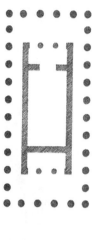

Morphological thinking, also called imaginative thinking by Rudolf Steiner, is thinking in forms, or pictures, the separate parts called forth out of one another as a mobile idea organism in time. The world of imagination is a world of perpetual transformation, one thing changing into another. Its images are not merely reflected by the physical-spiritual bodily organization as are spatial ideas, but absorbed like a seal in wax become a faculty of a perceiving thinking.[2]

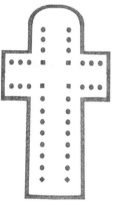

## Writing This Book

The inspiration to write this book arose from the author's four-year stay at the Goetheanum. A daily discourse with the building's presence gradually became encapsulated on the page and the loose pages gradually incorporated into a bound form.

In the following, the author explores a sensorial exact imagining the Goetheanum. The method ventured is a personal exploration observing and sketching to discover the idea of the building. The approach is based on Johann Wolfgang von Goethe's way of phenomenology: to think the phenomenon

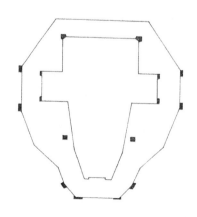

*Caryatid from the
Acropolis at Athens*

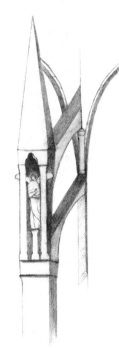

*Reims Cathedral
—flying buttress*

*Chartres Cathedral
—flying buttress*

in imagination, letting the phenomenon's relationships disclose its intrinsic nature. To participate in such a conversation with the building is at best a lover's cryptic divining. It is hoped, however, that the perception of the Goetheanum turned in the phrase of the written page may elicit an inkling of appreciation for the realm the Goetheanum opens up. The present study is a search for a language to portray the living language of the building's architecture.

The language of imagination points to the defining interplay between self and world, of the act of thinking congruent with nature. What Samuel Taylor Coleridge called in "Dejection: An Ode," "my shaping spirit of Imagination," reads, or interprets, the sense phenomena perceiving anew the given. The act of imagination is creative of consciousness in transforming thought into image. Imagination transforms abstraction into image and lifts the concept of transitory objects to the eternal life of the spirit. The life of things are their own meaning and the life of imaginative thinking their voice. Metamorphosis reveals this meaning as the language of imagination.

The title of this book refers not only to Goethe's way of imaginative perception with its primacy of experience in a "delicate empiricism" (Goethe), but to Coleridge's way of thought: *polar logic*. Coleridge championed this term and possibly coined it based on his readings of Giordano Bruno. It refers to the mode of imaginative thinking as the predicate for creativity. Such thinking derives its creative faculty from the reciprocal interpenetration of interacting ideas, principles, or forces. The synthesis of opposites begets the new—Logos logic of a creative trichotomy in its aspect of communicative intelligence. It is this principle that may be seen to underlie the architecture of the Goetheanum's *double-space* motif.

*The Drawings* in this book are by the author. They were conceived as studies. Their purpose is to aid perception of the building.

*The Umbra Study* of the Goetheanum is drawn in the corner of the right hand pages. These drawings depict the movement of the shadows on the building followed in the course of one day (on the whole in half hour increments) from sunrise (6:00) to sunset (21:20) when the sun was at its

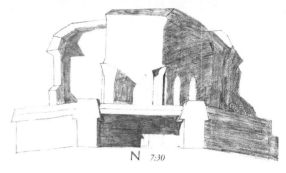

N 7:30

peak during the week of Saint John (the last week of June). (The June sun shines on the north face of the building from approximately 6:00 to 10:00; on the east face of the building from 6:15 to 14:00; on the south face of the building from 8:00 to 19:00; on the west face of the building from 10:30 to 21:20; and again on the east face of the building from 19:30 to 21:00.)

Shadows define a spatial form. The shadows change in the course of the day allowing for the eye's interest to continually engage in their movement. The building acts as both shadow thrower and screen for the image projection, and it is not without interest which parts of the building play the corresponding roles. As the light source changes and the cast shadows play across the building, the forms reveal in the source of this movement an imagination. The rising sun with its increasing light and its new and fresh impulse draws us out and spurs us on to the activity of the day. The setting sun with its decreasing light and its warm, inward, reflective glow draws us back into ourselves. The will-awakening morning light plays across the east face of the Goetheanum as well as partially the north and south faces. The thought-descending evening light plays across the west face of the Goetheanum as well as the south and north faces. The umbra movement across the Goetheanum may be viewed as an exact imagination of a sundial of the world in its soul nature.

Across the symmetry of the east and west faces of the building, the sun brings an asymmetry (except for the brief moment when the sun is due east and due west). This play of asymmetry with symmetry creates freedom within lawfulness illuminating variation within balance.

The shadow of a human being throws light. Rudolf Steiner: "Because the relation between spirit and physical is reversed, a clairvoyant can see the spirit, which a human being has as inner illumination, in his or her shadow."[3] The umbra forms of the Goetheanum may confer a like aspect and may play an illuminating role in the building.

The presentation of these umbra drawings accompany the reader throughout the book or can be flipped through to access their inherent movement. At the back of the book, the sequence of umbra drawings is presented again in an overview compiled across two pages.

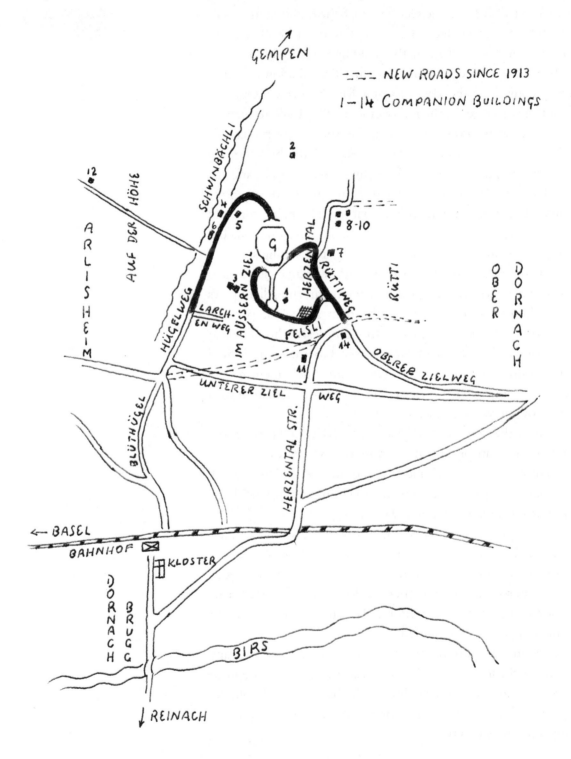

# DORNACH AND THE GOETHEANUM HILL

GEMPEN

---- NEW ROADS SINCE 1913
1—14 COMPANION BUILDINGS

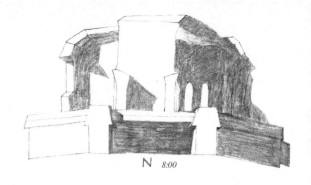

N *8:00*

# 2

# *The Three Paths*

## *Baptism*

On old Dornach Gemeinde (town district) maps prior to 1913, the hill where the Goetheanum stands in a little corner of Switzerland was named *Herzenthal* (heart-valley). For the first topographical drawings for the new project on the hill, the location's name was briefly used to designate the project differently written *Herzenthal, Herzental,* or simply *Herztal.* The name *Johannesbau* was then transferred from the initial building conception in Munich. The name was given by those in charge of the project, the Johannesbau Verein (the Johannes Building Association) after the character Johannes Thomasius in Rudolf Steiner's mystery plays. The production of the mystery plays was the impetus for building a theater in which to perform them. The name *Goetheanum* was finally arrived at in 1918 on Rudolf Steiner's indications: "I would greatly prefer to give the name 'Goetheanum' to the building at Dornach which is devoted to that 'spiritual research' [...which] I would love to give the name 'Goetheanism' to."[4] Thus, a name for the home for anthroposophy changed three times developing its essence from the human heart to characterize the quality of the land, to an individual character in the plays for which the building was built, to finally, honoring Goethe, the metamorphic thinking inherent in the architectural forms of the building.

HERZTAL
PROIEKT *Mai 1913*

*Herzenthal*
*Projekt*
*22 Juni 1913*

HERZENTAL
PROIEKT
*15 Juli '13*

*Johannesbau*
*September 1914*

GOETHEANUM

*Three Routes* lead to the Goetheanum traversing in unique ways the terrain of the hill relating in individual ways to the building. The three routes were laid out on what were existing field paths prior to the evening of 20 September 1913 when the foundation stone to the commencement of building was laid on an open hill. Prior to 1913, the stretch of Hügelweg past Unterer Zielweg (today Goetheanum Strasse) was a dirt access road to a reservoir where it then petered out to a footpath that continued in a straight line toward the Gempen. Rüttiweg, a farmer's field track prior to 1913, cut around the fields to end in the field behind what is today the Holzhaus. Even the beginnings of the Felsli (cliff) footpath were indicated. A pre 1913 path branched off from Rüttiweg to continue up the east side of the Felsli where even today an unofficial way is trampled. These old field paths were used in their initial directions, extended in bends past the Heating House (see map, 5), short of the de Jaager House (7), and west at the Felsli to curve toward the new building on the hill.

A grand, royal road led single and straight to the great architectural structures of past ages. Three small routes curve indirectly toward the Goetheanum. In contrast to the sacred buildings of the past, the approach to the Goetheanum must be found, chosen, and followed upon with uncertainty as the different paths circle in their different ways the hill's crowning summit.

The experience of approach to the Goetheanum is not unlike the experience of walking a labyrinth such as at Chartres or Knossos in Crete. Such labyrinths are images of the long, confusing, and potentially fatal losing of the thread of the soul's path to the spirit. The path into the labyrinth is the path out of the cosmos into creation. In the empty center of the labyrinth, one's identity is found. The return journey proceeds traversing with the thread of imaginative thinking the way through the labyrinth of sense-based thought to the spirit.

In the approach to the Goetheanum, it is not evident where the different routes lead. Each route passes by or turns away from the building providing no shortcut or more direct way that might hasten the journey. In this sense, the Goetheanum is the empty center dependent for its yielding intent on the transformative journey toward the inner alignment of spirit.

*Hügelweg* prior to 1913 was named Brugg (bridge). The route leads from the bridge that crosses over the Birs River into the town of Dornach, or Dornach Brugg. Dornach Brugg was for a long time a small village at the river crossing for its sister village further up the hill, Ober Dornach. Hügelweg leads up the north side of the hill paralleling the Schweinbach stream (earlier named Schwinbachli for its characteristic of disappearing [verschwinden] in underground channels).

N  *8:30*

Prior to 1913, Hügelweg was a dirt footpath for the townsfolk on the hill, mostly farmers, to make their way on Sundays to the Franciscan cloister down the hill. This narrow stretch of the route was for a while named Bluthügelweg in memory of the battle fought as part of the independence for the Swiss Confederation. The Goetheanum hill and the field above it, In den Goben, was the center of the battle fought on 22 July 1499 that gave rise to the name Bluthügel (Blood Hill).

Today, following this path, the first view of the Goetheanum is from the building's grounds past the small road called Lärchenweg. The Goetheanum grounds open up for the most part the close views of the building while distant perspectives of the building may be glimpsed from strategic open spaces in the Birs River valley or from the surrounding hills. At the corner to Lärchenweg, a partial view of roof and front flank of the building loom obscurely above and behind the Halde/Brodbeck House (drawing 1).

*Hügelweg: Drawing 1*

Rudolf Steiner designed the Halde as an annex for eurythmy. The Brodbeck House is the original house on the hill, which Steiner later renovated. There he spent his first night on the hill and made the discovery of the land. Next to the building is a pine grove, which eventually became the resting place for his ashes. Behind the grove, the Goetheanum is intimated, perched high up, carefully protected, and veiled by branches (drawing 2).

The road continues along the field below the Halde, the Halde dominating the steep incline. Behind the Halde through the trees, a portion of the Goetheanum can be glimpsed. Past the reservoir, the stark north wall of the east part of the building is seen (drawing 3).

*Hügelweg: Drawing 2*

*Hügelweg: Drawing 3*

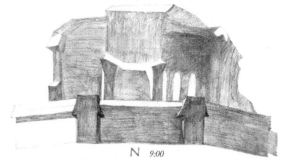

The cedars that hide the northwest portion of the building, as with the pines around the Goetheanum, were planted during the building period at the request of the Arlesheim town council to block the view of the building from Arlesheim. The Goetheanum Building Association responded with planting a slow-growing tree: cedars. Without the cedars, the view would fall grandly on the full north façade. Abreast of the building, continuing along the road, the entire length of the building is measured and the greater part of the north façade opens up to view (drawing 4).

*Hügelweg: Drawing 4*

The upper part of the large sloping field from the Halde to the Heating House is steeply sloped due to the earthwork to extend the level ground for the building site from the soil dug for the foundation.

*Hügelweg: Drawing 5. Above the road, the Goetheanum sits like a fortress.*

To the left, the road passes the Glass House, where the colored windows for the Goetheanum were cut, and the Publishing House for the Anthroposophic Press of Marie and Rudolf Steiner. To the right, it passes the Heating House, which originally housed a coal furnace to heat the Goetheanum (drawing 6).

*Hügelweg: Drawing 6*

These are all buildings designed by Rudolf Steiner and dedicated to the construction, activities, and functioning of the Goetheanum. The quince apple trees with their hard fruit around the Glass House and the hazelnut trees with their warmth and water-absorbing activity around the Heating House were planted at his request to balance the activities in those buildings.[5]

Then, with the east face of the building visible, the road finally curves toward the Goetheanum (drawing 7).

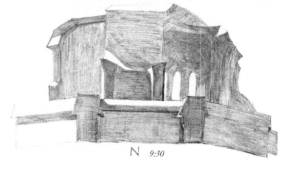

N   9:30

*Hügelweg: Drawing 7*

The approach to the east façade is symmetrical. However, there is little space for the road to straighten out for the experience of symmetry to be met with equilibrium. An early map shows plans to curve the road further out from the building allowing for a longer straight approach. This initial plan was discarded in favor of the closer bend. The strong bend in the approach is short and dynamic, the grade steep, and the moment of symmetry brief (drawing 8).

*Hügelweg: Drawing 8*

*Hügelweg: Drawing 9*

With this dynamic, the contrast of the east face of the building is heightened: a picture of a quiet, severe, and lofty elevation (drawing 9). Originally, no side relief pillars (pilasters) nor protruding roofline (cornice) were intended on the east side of the building, but the corners simply beveled, which would have given a clear cubic block form with a greater sense of solidity and repose.

At the east side, there is no public access to enter the building, only the stage door. To seek the front main entrance, the second half of the building is measured up close from back to front to complete a full circumnavigation of the building.

Hügelweg, *the way up the hill,* accesses the mountain citadel by pacing out the fullness of the building plan, whose proportions are taken from front to back and then mirrored up close from back to front. The building is circled, fully encompassed, and fully objectified. The will is addressed in the steep rise of ground and curve of the road. In the abrupt confrontation of the east side's symmetry, the plain façade is severe. And the artist's door is accessed for the stage to perform plays of initiation.

*Rüttiweg* was originally named Herzentalweg for the valley in which it lies. It was the continuation of old Herzental Strasse. With the laying of the Goetheanum Strasse and Dorneck Strasse, it received its own name, Rüttiweg. Rüttiweg is named for land south of the road. *Rütt* means cultivating wild brush and forested land for agriculture and reminds us of the famous Swiss oath. The Rütti-oath was sworn on the Rütti-field by the Vierwaltstättersee in 1291 and gave birth to the idea of an independent land and the founding of the Swiss Confederation.

Rüttiweg grades at a slight incline toward the south wing of the Goetheanum (drawing 1). A cherry and apple orchard slopes in a concave bowl up to the building. The vantage point at the juncture to Rüttiweg presents in full exposure the building's western flank and southern façade. It is most often the first impression the visitor receives on climbing the stretch of road from Herzental Strasse to Obererzielweg of the building rising above the Felsli outcrop. From this distance and three-quarter view, the building is presented in harmony above the gentle slope of orchard. The roofline falls precipitously in

*Rüttiweg: Drawing 1*

the west and gradually over the south wing. The windows rise vertically between the three-dimensional pillar and hollowed conjunction. The Goetheanum is harmoniously set on a green hill above crowns of trees. There, one makes the sudden discovery of this unique and astonishing building.

Rüttiweg initially proceeds toward the south wing of the Goetheanum only to veer gently away and then disappear entirely behind two tulip trees (drawing 2).

*Rüttiweg: Drawing 2*

*Rüttiweg: Drawing 3*

Indeed, it is hard to see from the beginning of Rüttiweg how one is to reach the Goetheanum. Eighty feet past the bend at the two tulip trees, Rüttiweg is three hundred feet from and parallel to the west entrance of the Goetheanum (drawing 3).

18

The road continues parallel to the Goetheanum. A freeness in the approach can be sensed in going alongside the building in contrast to the necessity felt in approaching the building directly.

Halfway along the building the road branches. The right fork continues the old field path. The left fork bends a hairpin turn to backtrack the front half-length of the building (drawing 4).

This curve by the de Jagger House faces directly the south portal hidden over the high bank of the road. Proportion and balance can be sensed in the coming together of the west and east parts of the building.

The five or six walnut trees along the south bank on the edge of the cherry field were planted on Rudolf Steiner's indications. Steiner hoped that the students in the eurythmy training, located in the temporary carpenter shop, would pick up the nuts from the ground in autumn and in the bending over gesture connect with the earth. The birch trees are also an indication of Rudolf Steiner's. The birch tree absorbs well the lead from car fumes, and the south entrance was the automobile drop off point to the building.[5]

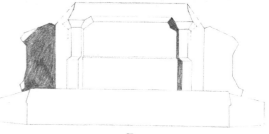

E  6:15

*Rüttiweg: Drawing 4*

19

The road curves toward the Goetheanum, accompanying it as a friend (drawing 5).

A first full-unencumbered view appears. As the road levels out and enters the precincts of the building, a sense of being its ward can be felt within its shadow. From behind and from the right, the west front entrance is approached.

Rüttiweg, the way of *cultivating* through the *valley of the heart,* is the path to the culture of the open heart. Initially, its way is directed parallel to the building relating freely to it, which is the cardinal, moral impulse in meeting another in allowance and furtherance of another's freedom. Then, in accompanying the building, the quality of approach becomes one of companionship, of going alongside, in-hand with the other. The route turns parallel to the building's middle dynamically relating to the building's own turning. It addresses the characteristic of the world of the front half of the building. The evolving world of human beings and their discourse is walked on Rüttiweg.

*Rüttiweg: Drawing 5*

*The Felsli Path* shows up in the earliest topographical maps for the new project on the hill with Rudolf Steiner's signature. The path branches off from Rüttiweg to curve in a great S-shape toward the Goetheanum. From below the Felsli with its towering linden and oak trees, the Goetheanum is viewed from the southwest at a 45° angle to its axis and at a distance of five hundred feet. It rises out of foliage on a green hill (drawing 1).

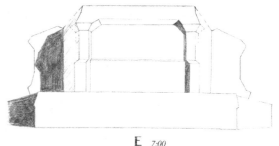

E  7:00

*Felsli path: Drawing 1*

It is not evident how the Goetheanum is to be reached as the Felsli path veers away from the building. Having faced the Goetheanum, the Felsli path turns its back on the building and curves in toward the rocks at the foot of the Felsli. In 1913, the Felsli outcrop was strikingly bare, a treeless mound of rock uncovering the earth. Today, oaks arch overhead as the path rises toward the clouds. As the path rounds the outcrop of stone to the right, a valley falls away to the left. As the path rises from out of the tree cover and straightens into the open light, to the left a cherry orchard slopes steeply, and to the right a bank of brush shoulders above. The view spreads out in a sweeping vista of the Birs River valley to the horizon of hills (drawing 2, over).

*Felsli path: Drawing 2*

The projection of the horizon encompasses the entire arc of the setting sun in the course of the year. The sun journeys from its winter solstice point, left above the southern arm of the Blauen hill with its castle ruin, to the summer solstice point, right above the woods and fields behind the town of Reinach on the other side of the Birs River from Dornach. The equinox point is the Landskron knoll. Accompanying this neck of the path is a waist-high wall that rises gradually from the Felsli to end halfway in a lay-by for a bench upon which to rest and view the distant perspective.

The path winds further leveling out to reenter the lofty tree cover of the upper edge of a small wood. It rounds the sculpted stone of the raised rondel and burrows out of the brush to finally turn toward and confront the Goetheanum in a wide arc. The Goetheanum is now viewed almost level from the northwest, close, and at a more intimate angle to its axis (drawing 3). The path curves in an embracing arc from the left to the entrance of the Goetheanum.

The Felsli path combines the two sides of the Goetheanum hill, Herzental and Im Ausseren Ziel. It is a synthesis of Rüttiweg and Hügelweg. Im Äussern Ziel (In Outer Aim) is the old local name for the area of the northwest incline of the Goetheanum hill below which Hügelweg runs. Herzental is the old local name for the valley to the south of the hill through which Rüttiweg runs. These names characterize the two roads

22

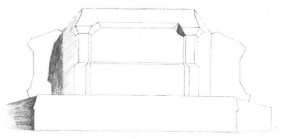

that lie in their terrain. The Goetheanum lies between the polarity of *outer* and *inner* locally named land. Due to its joining polarities, its frontal approach, and the importance that Rudolf Steiner placed on it, the Felsli path may be considered the main approach to the building.

However, in contrast to its importance, it is a small footpath. Indeed, it is initially invisible. Proceeding up Rüttiweg a hundred and fifty feet, the path appears suddenly and close, especially when the grass is tall, nor is it evident where this path leads. If one decides to try it, one will soon discover that it leads away from the building in a wide arc. Viewed from the middle of the arc, the Goetheanum appears unapproachable with no way to it, its base enclosed with trees on the hill's summit. To continue, one must turn one's back to the building and one's face to the cliff wall and the open sky. The sight of and direction to the Goetheanum must be abandoned and the valley of life that unfolds must be greeted. The path skirts the cliff wall. The panorama spreads out of the valley below like a

*Felsli path: Drawing 3*

great review on life. West with the setting sun is the direction of death. Life is the valley of death. The initial image of the unattained Goetheanum is carried into the world. To continue, the path must be followed into the shade of a grove of trees. Then between branches, fragments of the building are seen. The path opens up in a wide arc, and the building is at hand across a short field.

With the outer movements of a sailing boat tacking right, left, right, the Felsli path turns with the inner dynamics of the story of Parzival. In his search for the spirit and due to his purity of soul, Parzival innocently comes upon the Grail castle. However, due to his immaturity, he is thrust from its gates and must wander through the valley of the world with its trials of experience. Then, with the inner maturity of self-knowledge, he finds the Grail castle again.

On the Felsli path, the middle station (drawing 2) of the Birs River valley permits a pause between the two views of the building (drawings 1 and 3). To do so, one must forgo the visible presence of the building and the way sought without reference to it. The view of the Goetheanum is then carried as memory that may be freely worked with.

This straight ledge of the path is image for an existential drama. Without the visible presence of one's goal, one may forget failing to perceive the reality of one's pursuit. With nothing certain to hold on to, doubt takes hold, existence becomes uncertain, and one's relationship to the world is severed. Lost to oneself, the darkness of night ends with death and its question, what is death's nothingness—what is the human thing?

As image, the path provides the trial and likewise the solution. As the path skirts the valley, the gaze is directed out into the world. There, in the middle of life, in the great wide widths of the social fabric of life's variety, the meeting with the essence of the Goetheanum is viewed: life's path of trials leading to the recognition of one's fellows and the Parzival question, "What ails you?"

# 3

## *Forecourt, Rondel, and Allée*

*The west façade of the Goetheanum
viewed from the rondel.*

*The Forecourt* at the west portal of the building joins
the three paths together. The three paths meet: from the left
the Felsli path, from the right Rüttiweg, and from behind
Hügelweg. In front of the forecourt is an allée (an alley in a
park, bordered by trees or bushes) ending in a rondel. The
allée and rondel are an enclosed space entered only from the
forecourt. Just as other paths that had crisscrossed the hill prior
to 1913 have long since vanished, so today new paths and roads
have been added as access routes to particular portions of the
hill including a road that cuts into the rondel as an access route
to the Halde. However, as part of the entrance to the building,
the allée must be entered from the forecourt. Just as a spiritual
threshold requires a change, or turning, of consciousness, so
an architectural or landscape threshold (upon the paths, before
the hall of the auditorium, at the forecourt) requires a turn away

25

to proceed in the opposite direction. At the forecourt, a turn away from the building is necessary for the allée to be entered. Similarly, on exiting the building, the allée invites its entrance in a reverse procedure. The forecourt is a dynamic juncture to the entrance of the Goetheanum. The actual entrance is from the rondel.

*The Rondel* is the entrance to the Goetheanum and provides the finest view of the building. The rondel is cardinally placed on the axial line of the building with the building viewed in perfect symmetry and harmony. It is the only view from the entire surroundings of the building in perfect balance. Behind the rondel, a wood (currently protected) on a steep incline fully obstructs the view further to the west. The circular, enclosed space of the rondel holds one while the straight allée directs one's gaze to the building. Five benches designed by Rudolf Steiner edge the rondel and invite one to pause further in contemplation of this view of the building. The allée's length of two hundred feet plus the rondel and forecourt is three hundred and thirty feet, almost the building's entire length of three hundred feet. At the rondel, one is as distant from the building as the building itself is long. This view measures in its distance the building's length.

The harmony of the building in its vertical dimension conveys the entire structure as a column: the ground floor the base, the roof the capital. The proportion of its width to its height is a measure of two to one. That is, the width is twice the height. (The ground level width is two hundred and eighty feet; the second level width is two hundred and ten feet; their combined mean width is approximately the height of the building of one hundred and twenty-one feet [280 feet + 210 feet = 490 feet $\div$ 2 = 245 feet, which is approximately $2 \cdot 121$ feet, or 37 meters].) The harmony of its depth reveals through its isosceles trapezoid form the entire front half of the building fully visible and complete. A lightness lifts the building into the realm of an imagination—hardly a nine-story high building.

Viewed from the rondel, the axial symmetry of the building contrasts with the polar convex and concave forms of its placement in the land. The Gempen hill climbs away to the right, its limestone, glacially formed rock-cliff characteristic is

carried thematically into the outer design of the Goetheanum. The Ermitage valley falls away to the left. Its historical past in the Parzival epic and the Saint Odile chronicle is tied thematically to the inner function of the building.[6] Up on the Gempen, the wind can whip apace and stunt the gnarled cypresses, and the panoramic view can inspire ideas of great enterprise. In contrast, below in the Ermitage, a fountain trickles into a still pool before a cave, and the sober contemplations of self-analyses can reflect like shadows against the somber cave's walls. The Goetheanum is placed in this landscape of polar extremes as the balancing middle.

The isosceles trapezoid shape of the auditorium walls allows for the sides of the front half of the building to be visible from the rondel. The openness of and therefore the freedom toward the building are experienced due to this full visibility of the building's front half. Nothing is hidden, all is revealed.[7] In the frontal plane, the wingspan of the building sits back and extends the widths. This mantle-like gesture furthers the opening and welcoming inclusivity of the building. The front's verticality is emphasized by the symmetry of the building and the receding levels.

Southwest of the Goetheanum on top of the Felsli, Rudolf Steiner created a landscape of a series of seven semi-circular steps that lead to a circular platform. On the platform, a linden tree grows. Planted in 1908, it is today a mighty tree. The linden for hundreds of years has graced village greens imbuing with warmth and peace the healing quality of the heart to bond human beings in community. The axis line of the steps of the Felsli rondel is in direct line with the center of the allée's rondel, which in turn is in line with the Goetheanum. Both rondels have a diameter of sixty-nine feet (21 meters), the measure of the distance between the centers of the two cupolas of the first Goetheanum.[8] The allée's rondel synthesizes the polar spaces of the building's interior and the Felsli's exterior world of nature.

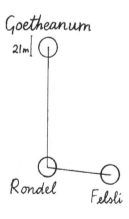

*The Allée* is the royal road of old. However, although it leads to the building, it must first be found. Although the goal is the building, at the forecourt one must first turn away from the building and proceed down the allée ending at the rondel. Only then, with a pivotal turn to the axial alignment of the building

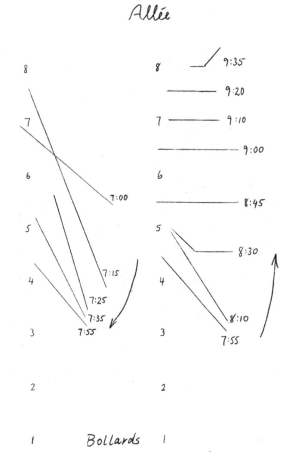

Allée

8

8        / 9:35

        — 9:20

7

7 ———— 9:10

      ———— 9:00

6

6

    7:00     ———— 8:45

5

5     ———— 8:30

4   7:15

4

  7:25      8:10

  7:35

3  7:55     3     7:55

2           2

1     Bollards   1

does the allée reveal its royal secret. Walking up the 5% grade of the allée, the proportions of the building change. With the shortening of the distance, the encounter with the building builds. From the stillness of concentration in the rondel to the engagement of the limbs to walk the allée, time is entered in a rhythmic sequence that builds with an increasing tempo of the changing proportions of the building. From the stationary contemplation standing in the rondel to the movement of the limbs in the active will of walking, the perfect harmony of the building's forms is transformed.

The forms of the building change in a progression of sequences. In the narrowing of the isosceles trapezoid, the experience of free will changes to necessity. In the increasing persistent encounter with the building, the path of self-knowledge of old is trod. The building asks; the answer is the self. It is the eternal question newly imagined. The question is the human being: what and who is this human being? The path of spiritual knowledge is the process of meeting this being. (A detailed portrayal of the allée is explored in chapter 5.)

The architect in charge of the first Goetheanum building, Carl Schmid-Curtius, in 1914 reported an indication of Rudolf Steiner's for periwinkle to wind around posts between the bollards like a caduceus. The gardener Antonie Ritter in 1920 reported an original intention of Rudolf Steiner's to plant roses along the allée along with other five-petaled flowers of the Rosaceae family in the west meadow, such as the plum trees. The caduceus symbol with the periwinkle's five-petaled blue flowers and the five-petaled red roses are flowers par excellence that express the human being's path of transformation of evil to good through self-knowledge.

Lastly, the umbra movements cast by the building onto the allée are of interest. From the rising sun, the building throws a shadow across the allée. As the sun rises, the shadow of the north side of the roofline initially travels down the allée. Then the shadow from the front of the roofline travels up the allée. The diagram left shows the umbra movements across the allée for the morning of the last day of June. In the evening, the warm glow of the setting sun raises the shadow from within the covered entrance until it disappears (see the sequence of changing shadows in the drawings on pages 107–121).

28

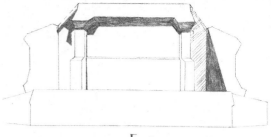

E  *11:00*

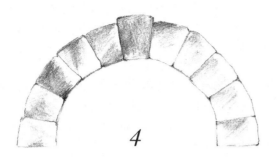

# 4

## *Pillar, Pediment, and Frieze*

*The Threshold* to great structures is heralded with a representation of watchful guardians to left and right of the entrance. The threshold demarcates a change of space and therewith a corresponding change in consciousness. A building's entrance or indeed any door requires a form that accords with the corresponding change intimating and preparing for as well as creating the change. The entrance forms of great structures reveal the evolving enigma of the threshold.

A pair of sphinxes crouched along the road before the ancient Egyptian temple to test the seeker after knowledge with a riddle. This enigmatic creature with emergent head from an amalgam of bull, lion, and eagle reflected the human being who in self-knowledge came to know these forces. Before the gate, a pair of obelisks stood upright. In Assyria, the sphinxes flanked the palace gate and were depicted as five-legged creatures standing frontally and walking in profile simultaneously.

In Mycenae within the corbel arch, a pair of lions reared up in the centering, the temporary construction space of an arch.

Ancient Rome's love affair with the arch, from engineering works to monuments, as the basis for vaults and domes, idealized its structure. An arch's keystone locks in place the weight of all its parts making the arch self-supporting. It coincided with Christ's life—the keystone spanning time.

In the medieval cathedral, a trumeau pillar with statue, often of the Savior, stands between the leaves of the central doorway supporting the lintel and arch above. Like the spine of a book that unites the pages, what unites also divides.

29

*Ruins of the stelea at Troy's Skaian Gate*

*Chartres Cathedral*

A sculptural asymmetry of the portal can be found in antiquity such as at ancient Troy where four stelae, pillar-like stone slabs, representing the gate-gods still stand outside the Skaian Gate to its right. Such an asymmetry is also encountered in the medieval cathedral. In Chartres Cathedral, the sculpture in the Royal Portal's left bay's tympanum represents the Ascension and in the right bay the Nativity. The middle bay depicts as synthesis the apocalyptic Parousia. Chartres Cathedral also presents a striking architectural asymmetry. Through a turn of its history, a Renaissance architect rebuilt the cathedral's west façade's north tower asymmetrical to its twin south tower.

*Jachin and Boaz* are the names given to the pillars that flanked the entrance to Solomon's Temple. The two syllables of Jachin translated are, "god" and "establish," or "with God's help to establish," or simply, "god's wisdom." Boaz translates, "in you is strength." The event is related in Chronicles: "And Solomon reared up the pillars before the temple, and called the name of that on the right hand Jachin, and the name of that on the left Boaz." Jachin was constructed to radiate light; Boaz was dark yet phosphorescent. With their enormous measure of 18 cubits high (31 feet) and 4 cubits wide (6.5 feet), 27 tons of bronze have been estimated as necessary for the four-finger-width wall of the hollow cylinder (not including its capital). Seen as attributes of the temple, Jachin was placed right, south of the entrance, and Boaz to the left, north of the entrance. The temple was aligned with the entrance in the east and the altar in the west—as were the ancient Greek temples.

*On Whitsun 1907,* Rudolf Steiner depicted two pillars at the Munich Congress. As leader of the German section of the Theosophical Society, which hosted the Society's annual festival, he took the occasion to give an artistic decoration to the hall with far-reaching consequences. As part of the décor, a red pillar was depicted in front of the stage on the left and a blue pillar on the right.

Rudolf Steiner explained to his audience the esoteric nature of these two pillars. The pillars represented the mysteries of the blood. The red column represented the red oxygenated blood—through the in breath of air—as the tree of knowledge

30

and the path of incarnation. The blue column represented the blue carbon dioxide blood as the tree of death as a consequence of incarnation, which through the path of self development must be transformed into the tree of life.

Rudolf Steiner inscribed on the pillars script characterizing the path of knowledge and the path of life. The initial letters of two words were written on the pillars: *J* on the red pillar and *B* on the blue pillar. Rudolf Steiner: "I do not have the authority to express these two words, but which mean: 'I am Who was, I am Who is, I am Who will be.'"[9] In Revelations this utterance is "I am Alpha and Omega." The goal is to intertwine the separate pillars to become one: *J-B*. The spirit was sought through the synthesis of these entrance forms. (This impulse renewed may be found in the second Goetheanum—developed below.)

The colors red and blue have physiological effects upon the eye in correspondence to the significance of the two pillar's union. Perception of red destroys blood and nerve cells in the eye stimulating the production of oxygen (life) to restore the damage. Perception of blue leaves the oxygen to combine with carbon. Carbonic acid has the effect of consciousness.[10]

Opposite these two pillars, a painting hung at the back of the hall displaying the pillars a second time. Around the hall hung the seven seals of the Apocalypse painted after sketches made by Rudolf Steiner. In the middle painting of the series was depicted the fourth seal in the Apocalypse (Chapter 10): "His feet were pillars of fire; and he set his right foot upon the sea, and his left foot on the earth." A rainbow bridges the pillars. In the midst of the rainbow are sun and cloud. These images portrayed a mighty angelic being who held forth a little book of knowledge to be ingested, the root of which is bitter labor but its fruit sweet communion (see page 107). These images of the being of the temple encompassed the space in front of and behind the assembled audience.

In a notebook entry late 1923, Rudolf Steiner sketched two capital forms for two pillars.[11] The two forms are polar prototypes: one opens up to the architrave (drawing left), and the other closes off (drawing right). Accompanying sketches indicate pentagonal capitals that accent their lower or upper part. These sketches leave the provocative question of their possible use in the second Goetheanum—before the stage?

E *12:30*

*J*

In pure thinking, you find
The self that can hold itself.

Transform thought to picture,
You experience the creating wisdom.

*B*

Condense feeling to light,
You reveal the forming strength.

Objectify will to being,
So you create in world existence.

*After a sketch by Rudolf Steiner*

## Triune Pillar

The second Goetheanum may be seen to combine both symmetrical and asymmetrical elements in its entrance structure. The entrance forms integrate with the building the qualities of the symmetry plane (left/right) and the asymmetry of the frontal plane (back/forward). The entrance forms herald the building's ground motif of inner identity through polarity.

In the lower aperture, three doors are placed in a concave recess. A heavy lintel spans its length held by two supports. These relief pillars are asymmetrical: the inner half extends the shape of the lintel; the outer part conforms to the shape of the wall. The asymmetry of these pillar forms creates a movement dynamic to the balancing form of the entrance lintel.

Further out along the base are two symmetrical relief pillars, like the posts for the north and south entrances, with an isosceles trapezoidal form for its capital. However, unlike the front-facing pillars of the north and south portals, these pillars are angled out in the west portal. They function like hinges for the entrance. In the west, the building opens and the base angles out like a double door that is flush in the middle and is hinged on the outer two sides.

The isosceles trapezoid motif pillars at the outer end of the portal and the asymmetrical pillars at the inner end of the portal form together a great two-winged gate opening from inside out.

Exactly between and above these two pillars is the three-dimensional pillar in the second level. It soars to join inwardly the wall of the auditorium and outwardly the roof.

These three distinct pillar forms may be imagined to function as a single triune pillar to the left and right of the building's entrance—like a colossal order in classical architecture, which spans as an entrance form the building's façade.

Rudolf Steiner spoke of these three forms in introducing the building motif on 1 January 1924. The emphasis was on the three-dimensional pillar on the second level. The first level forms were less clearly defined, "like roots" from which the second level form developed.

The interpretive view of the forms of the west façade developed in the following is used to help characterize the quality of these forms. It is offered as one approach.

32

*The E-Ah-O* (German IAO) sound gesture sequence has its workbench in eurythmy, the movement art form that Rudolf Steiner created. The E-Ah-O eurythmy exercise is used often to begin and end an eurythmy class. That is to say, it is used as an entry and exit exercise to the eurythmic space. The E-Ah-O exercise plus a form to characterize Lucifer and Ahriman were the first sound gestures and forms that Rudolf Steiner gave at the beginnings of the development of eurythmy in Munich in August 1912.

E  *14:00*

The painting of the E-Ah-O in the large cupola of the first Goetheanum was placed center front before the entrance to the small cupola of the stage upon which initiation would be artistically played—although circumstances never allowed it.

The triune pillar of the Goetheanum may be seen to characterize the E-Ah-O spoken from the back to the front of the building coming toward the viewer. The great three-dimensional pillar in the middle level of the building may be seen to stand in the eurythmy sound gesture of "e" (German "i"). It holds the balance between the two pillars in the lower level. Rudolf Steiner was particularly concerned for the pillar's exact execution. Its three-dimensional, independent verticality holds a dynamic balance: its inner side anchors down into the upward lift of the auditorium wall—overcoming its separateness; its outer side lifts to support the weight of the roof—in service.

The pillar with the isosceles trapezoid motif capital may be seen to stand in the eurythmy sound gesture of "ah" (German "a"). The pillar's form is self-contained and stands sentry like a great Tau-cross (T) form. It is instrumental in the force to split open the front of the building acting as a hinge for the opening aperture of the building's entrance. In addition, it is geometrically symmetrical carrying the idea as lawful origin, as alpha, of the building. It reveals as archetype both the load and lift motif for the building and the ground plan idea of the isosceles trapezoid and square. The blueprint idea of the building is the seed that opens the building.

The inner asymmetrical relief pillars may be seen to stand in the eurythmy sound gesture of "o." The pillar asymmetrically embraces wall and lintel in an inclusionary gesture. It reaches in to carry the lintel in a gesture of the great affirmative "Yes"

33

of love to give entrance. It reaches out to join the lift of the wall. Its horizontal furthest forward placement in the building embracing the entrance is balanced with the gesture of invitation into the building. The *E* and *O* pillars asymmetrically support wall (lift) and lintel/roof (load) but do so in reverse direction to each other. *Ah* opens the building and *O* embraces us, the *E* (the "I am") in each of us.

The triune pillar of the Goetheanum may be seen to represent in dynamic form the Christ, "I am Alpha and Omega," the E-Ah-O as guardian of the threshold. The pillars carry within each side the duality in the frontal plane (back/ forward axis), *Ah* and *O*, which is overcome in a higher unity, *E*. On crossing the threshold to the spiritual world, whether in initiation or in initiation's image of a sacred building, the human being meets in self-knowledge the two beings of duality. Elevated above these opposites is that force which combines the world-duality into divine unity: "I am the door." A three- fold activity of balance may be seen to be placed left and right of the entrance of the Goetheanum to awaken in those who enter a free relating in balance between representations of the Being of balance. (Drawings of the E, Ah, and O eurythmy figures designed by Rudolf Steiner, and the E-Ah-O triune pillar are on the back cover.)

### The Pediment

The roof as seen in the model of the building (see drawing, page 135) is composed of 28, or 4 x 7, straight-edged, faceted surfaces divided into four main parts: 1) The front; 2) A raised protrusion sandwiched between front and auditorium; 3) The auditorium plus wings; 4) The stage.

Unlike Rudolf Steiner's model for the Goetheanum, the constructed building does not, regrettably, differentiate the roofline between stage and auditorium. The decision to alter the model's design was taken in the belief that the technical demands of the stage required its extra height. Although not documented, it must be assumed that Rudolf Steiner gave Ernst Aisenpreis, the architect in charge of the building, permission for this change.

From the rondel, the roof's front, protrusion, and wings of the auditorium are visible. These three partitions of the

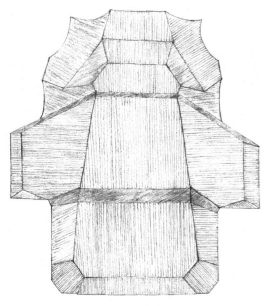

*Drawing of the roof from the model of the second Goetheanum*

roof are dynamically related in their gesture form. The front slants forward and down, the protrusion presses up, and the wings expand back and outward. These differentiated facets of weight reveal the life of the ground plan.

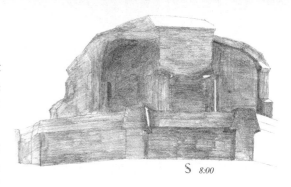

The triune E-Ah-O gestures may be seen in this movement of the forms of the Goetheanum's roof. It may be compared to the word of the macrocosm spoken in its capacity as pressure of world-sustaining and ordering being (drawing on back cover).

An examination of the sculpture in the pediments of Greek temple architecture is revealing. The pediments placed in the front and back triangle of the roof depict the world of the gods. For example, in the Parthenon, the theme of the pediment in the west is the contest between Athena and Poseidon for the patronage of Athens and in the east the birth of Athena. The weight-bearing load of the roof is the expression of the macrocosm of the gods.

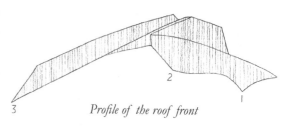

*Profile of the roof front*

## The Frieze

The meeting of roof and wall in the roofline of the Goetheanum may be compared to the frieze of the ancient Greek temple. The frieze that winds around the Greek temple between roof and wall depicts the hero or human being in relation to the gods. The human being as pillar bears the gods as roof creating a place for divine worship represented in the frieze. In the Parthenon, it is the Panathenaic procession to honor Athena with the peplos (the garment representing the aura of the goddess). The procession's tremendous movement progresses contrasting prancing horses with serene riders.

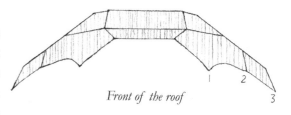

*Front of the roof*

The roofline movement in the Goetheanum has three points where movement is arrested. This cessation of movement occurs in shifts of direction. Three times an outward north/south movement is stopped by a contrary perpendicular west/east movement. Three times a downward movement is stopped by an upward movement. Three times the load of the roof is stopped by the lift of the wall. Each time the pressure of the meeting of roof and wall differs and develops its theme: 1) The front of the roof falls away to the sides, its forward, downward movement arrested by an upward lift of the angle shift from the front to the side of the building; 2) The molding line between roof and wall curves in a double curve from the

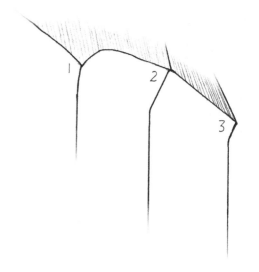

first point to the three-dimensional pillar; there, a point presses out where the movement is broken again in a surface direction shift from outward to upward along the building; 3) Behind this upward movement of the three-dimensional pillar, the mighty roof span of the auditorium falls out and down, to be brought to a halt by the wings. This point of the cessation of movement is the furthest outward and backward reach of roof and wall.

These three points formed by the cessation of movement may also be seen as the E-Ah-O gesture: the forward point *O*, the upward point *E,* and the outward point *Ah*. This dynamic meeting of load and lift utters the E-Ah-O word in its capacity as world-evolving transformer (drawing on back cover).

These three points join with the three front parts of the roof: the forward embracing part, the upward, pressed-out island, and the wide, extending auditorium/wings to continue the theme of the pillars below. The unifying, informing principle of the building may be considered as the E-Ah-O motif. This motif occurs three times in three different parts of the building: 1) The pillars; 2) The roof; 3) The meeting of pillar and roof. Comparing these parts to ancient Greek architecture, they represent the function of load and lift in accordance with: 1) The human being; 2) The macrocosm; 3) The meeting of the human being and macrocosm. The E-Ah-O motif may be seen to permeate the building's front half specific to each part.

The E-Ah-O motif is also expressive of the I in its threefold capacity as a thinking I, a feeling I, and a willing I. Rudolf Steiner describes its representation in color in the east end of the large cupola of the first Goetheanum: the human I directs its gaze out to the widths of the light-filled space up to the vault of heaven: the transparent, light-filled thinking I; it directs its gaze to the horizontal plane with all its movement of the sense world (such as the wind in the trees): the feeling I; it directs its gaze down to the fruits of the earth: the willing I.[12]

The I is the great integrator summing the parts reconciling polar opposites.

The Goetheanum is the house for the human being, the anthropos, in its wisdom-filled person, Sophia. The E-Ah-O motif heralds an architecture for a building built for the community of individuals: Anthroposophia.

# *5*

## *The West Façade*

### *The Three Apertures*

From the rondel, the west façade of the Goetheanum is
viewed: three front-facing apertures rise and recede back in the
three levels of the building. These three apertures define the
three levels. The lower aperture is concave, rectangular, and
framed with convex pillar, lintel, and step. It presents three
doors to enter the building. The upper aperture is convex,
framed with concave curves. It presents a single opaque
window—its color and engraved image seen only from within
the building. The lower and upper apertures are polar opposites
of each other, not only in form but also in function. The will to
walk toward and pull open the door is met and balanced with a
concave space surrounded with convex structures. The opaque
window—its mystery revealed only from within as the mystery
of initiation—is balanced with convex forms and flanked with
concave planes.

The middle-level aperture is a very large, almost square,
transparent window. It frames a glass door to the terrace. Two
smaller windows flank its sides. The regularity of the three
apertures in the lower level is modified to irregularity of their
size in the middle level. The solitary aperture in the upper level
is maintained by the emphasis of the large main window in
the middle level, yet modified by the inclusion of the two side
windows. The middle aperture combines both functions of
window and door of the lower and upper levels. Unlike the
upper level, the middle-level window is transparent allowing
perception of the world outside. Unlike the lower level, the

middle-level glass door allows restricted access to the intimate enclosure of the terrace. Five surfaces angle toward the great square window. They combine to form a cubic space behind the window, a dome-like space above, and a space for the sweep of the dual stairs in which are the two lobe-like smaller windows.

From the rondel, the threefold function of the levels in the front may be seen as a picture of the human being. The third level is a convex center, the head surrounded by expansive concavity, a cosmos of thought. The second level is a great convex center, the heart and lungs open to and in exchange with the world allowing both sense-perception via the windows and willed movement via the door. The first level is receptive will of a concave space surrounded by objective will of the convex and angled pillars and lintel.

To this threefold aspect as a picture of the human being is added the quality of how this picture holds itself, its stance, or gait. First, the levels advance, each forward from the one above. Second, the isosceles trapezoid walls of the auditorium converge. These qualities express well the forward-striding human being in Rudolf Steiner's sculpture, the Representative of Humanity (see chapter 14).

### The Fourteen + Four Bollards

Seven equally spaced bollards, ornamental stone posts, or way stones, on each side of the allée define its border and divide its length. These stones, designed by Rudolf Steiner for the first Goetheanum, are roughly fourteen-sided surfaces running into one another, asymmetrically shaped, and placed angled a fraction inward toward the allée. At the forecourt, two larger bollards on each side of the allée symmetrically shaped are placed angled clearly away from the building. These stone markers lend the allée a megalithic quality. They give spatial orientation to the changing coordinates of the building encountered in an individual, temporal step-by-step progression up the allée. The stones are spaced twenty-five feet apart, the measure of the allée's width. Seven measures, equal in length and width, divide the allée. Including the rondel, forecourt, and entrance, ten measured spaces, or stages, are passed through as one walks toward the Goetheanum.

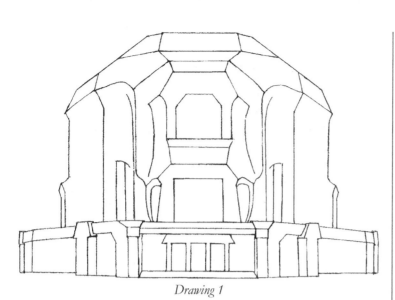

*Drawing 1*

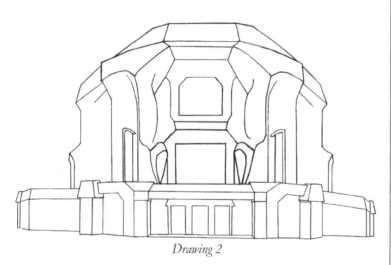

*Drawing 2*

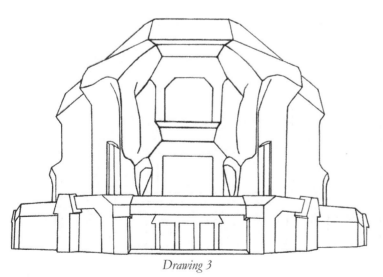

*Drawing 3*

S *8:45*

## A Sequence of Ten— the Human Being

From the rondel, the Goetheanum is viewed in the perfect harmony of its elements (drawing 1). The roofline is unified. The three pillar forms, called in this book E-Ah-O, are equally spaced. The three levels with the fourth level of the roof are of equal measure. The three receding side portions are in harmonious balance. The base level supports the column of the building. All is in its place. The architectural element of load is everywhere caught up by the element of lift in rhythmic unfolding. The base level supports to enclose, yet equally to widen out. The second level breathes with the cavities of windows and column spaces. The third level unifies as it joins with the roof in differentiated ways. Above all, the three planes of space are in perfect harmony.

From the first bollard, the view of the *E* pillar lifts above the roofline of the wings separating out from the unity of the roof. Equally, the *E* pillar separates out from the middle position between the *Ah* and *O* pillars and moves in the direction of the *O* pillar. The weight of the base level increases (drawings 2, 3, and 4).

39

Walking from the fourth to the fifth bollards, one reaches the middle point of the allée (drawings 5 and 6). Exactly halfway along the allée, the open and free quality allowed by perceiving the isosceles trapezoid sides of the building is lost. Till the middle, the trapezoid walls of the auditorium converged. Crossing the midpoint of the allée, the frontal (back/forward) plane of the building (the auditorium's walls) is lost and the horizontal (above/below) plane dominates. The experience of free will in the depth dimension is lost leaving a sense of necessity that increasingly becomes perceived in an above/below lopsided contortion of extremes.

From the sixth bollard, the tempo change of the perceived building's relationships markedly increases and the architectural elements of lift and load reverse: to lift above and load below. The extremes of lift, or lightness, of the three-dimensional pillar and the encasing, looming load, or weight, of the entrance visually split the building (drawings 7 and 8).

From the forecourt's middle, in line with the two larger bollards, the view of the building is fully split (drawing 9). Above and falling back and away, the lift element dominates. The roof with its element of load is no longer visible. The entire upper levels are within the margins of the lower level. Below, the entrance rectangle thrusts the heavy lintel

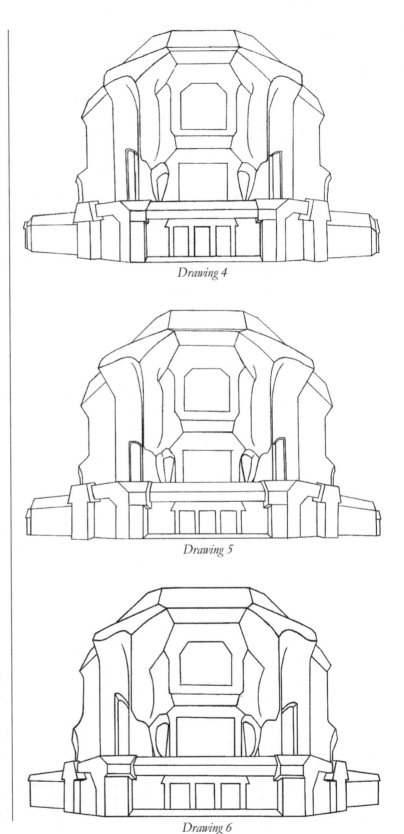

*Drawing 4*

*Drawing 5*

*Drawing 6*

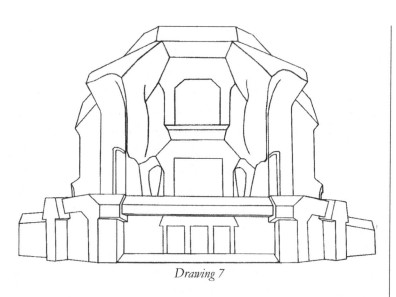

*Drawing 7*

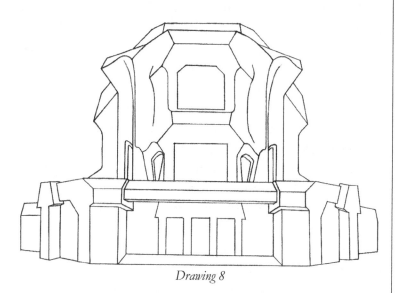

*Drawing 8*

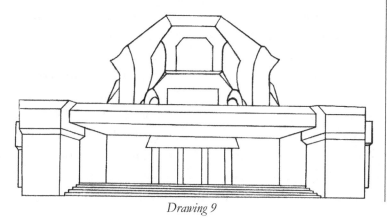

*Drawing 9*

forward supported by the massive block pillars. There below and wrenched forward, the element of weight massively intrudes. The middle element of the middle level that harmonized the two extremes is no longer present. The forms of the architecture have an adamant and admonishing effect constraining one's step.

On entering the rectangular portal, climbing the five steps, and pulling open the door (an interior space protects itself), the outer orientation of form retreats. Unassuming, without compelling, almost unwelcoming, the architectural elements allow for the free moment of entrance. Without orientation and alone, the threshold must be crossed.

## Christ and Michael

To leave the sanctuary of the rondel with its harmonious view of the building and proceed up the allée is to commit to a journey of dynamic change, a process that will lead to the greatest possible disharmonious view of the building. The changing depth plane brings about new relationships throwing the horizontal plane into disorder.

From the rondel, the architectural elements of the building may be seen as analogous to the striding figure in the sculpture, the Representative of Humanity. In walking the allée to encounter this being, a process of transformation occurs in the experience of balance crossing the allée's fulcrum. Crossing this midpoint, the perception of the architectural elements of the building reverse: from weight above and lift below to the experience of lift above and weight below. From the forecourt, the architectural elements of the building may be seen as analogous to the duality of Lucifer and Ahriman, the two beings present at the threshold of consciousness. The allée may be seen as the path uniting the individual to the context of the event that the sculpture portrays enacting in movement the dynamics of what is represented in the sculpture.

The drawings left are after a sketch by Edith Maryon from Rudolf Steiner's description on the 17 December 1922 of the Archangel Michael. Maryon wrote under the sketch: "Michael receiving the intelligence of human beings and carrying it to the gods (left). From the west (above)." This Michael gesture may be experienced on the west façade of the second Goetheanum in its witnessing, awaiting, and awakening gesture.

Rogier van der Weyden represented the Archangel Michael and Christ together in his Altarpiece of the Last Judgement (1452) like brothers, the Archangel Michael as emissary of Christ (drawing below left). In contrast, the portrayal Rudolf Steiner gives them is very different than their Renaissance depiction. Their joint activity manifests not in judgement but in holding open the entrance in a mood of expectancy.

Finally, individual and social aspects unite. On the one hand, the allée may be compared to the Mercury staff, or caduceus, a light staff entwined by a black and white snake. It symbolizes the development of the I through knowledge gained in overcoming evil through strength for the good.

On the other hand, the social aspect may be illustrated with the image of another exiting the building at the same time as one proceeds up the allée from the rondel. Both would meet in the middle of the allée. Such a meeting may be experienced as a meeting with the building in its essential aspect of promoting the meeting of individuals.

Then, in the entrance of the building, one is alone.

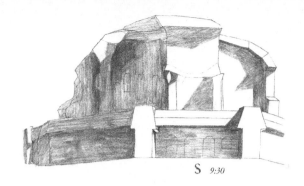

S  *9:30*

# 6

## Six and Seven

### A Sequence of Six and Seven—the Base

A drawing by Rudolf Steiner of the profile base of the building shows the six segments of the base like mathematical proportions of musical intervals.

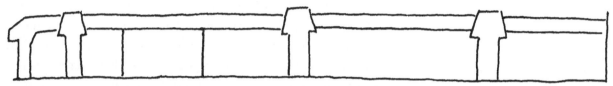

*After a sketch by Rudolf Steiner*

The following six drawings depict the building from the center of each of these side segments, or panels. The six views progress in a sequence of rhythmic differentiation. To walk along the side of the building viewing it is to experience a sequence of an unfolding progression, harmonious yet dramatic. If the front and back of the building are included, then there are two times seven sections of the building's base.

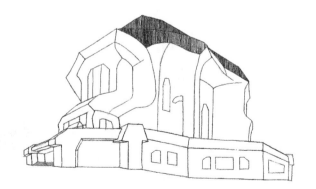

## South and North Entrances

Facing the north or south entrance is to powerfully encounter the asymmetric dynamic of the building. East is the enclosed stage, west the expressive auditorium. The polarity of stage and auditorium meet in the north and south entrance of the transept wings. The forces of this polarity are held together in harmony by the extension of the transept, the motif pillars, and the free-formed relief pillars in the second level. The motif pillars in the north and south entrances do not angle out as in the west entrance but face front giving them symmetry in themselves. The two motif pillars firmly present the ground plan of isosceles trapezoid and square exactly where these two aspects of auditorium and stage meet in the building. The north and south transept entrances, flanked by the motif pillars, establish the lawful meeting of the two halves of the building.

## A Sequence of Seven—the Auditorium

John James in *Chartres* shows the cathedral's measurements of the crossing of nave and transept have proportion 7:6. "The long axis of Understanding is Christ's, while the cross axis of Knowledge is Mary's. For Christ said: 'I am the Way,' while Mary was the patron of all philosophy. The long axis should contain the Perfect number in its ratio (6), just as Christ is the Perfect Man, while the transept axis should contain 7, for philosophy was her special prerogative as patron of the Liberal Arts."[13] The quality of the number seven may be seen to characterize the external forms of the Goetheanum's auditorium.

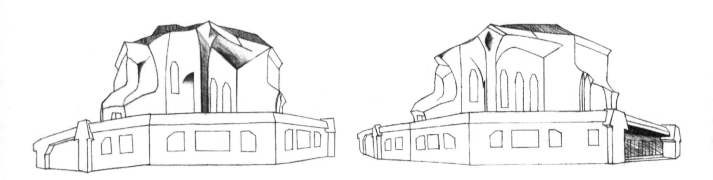

In the second Goetheanum, the three-dimensional pillar (4 in diagram) is radically positioned in the middle of polar forms. Flanking the upper level opaque window is a small convex three-sided pyramidal form (1 in diagram). Mirroring this and polar in form is the enormous, three-sided, concave extension of the expanse of auditorium wall that joins the wall of the wing and the roof over the light court (7 in diagram).

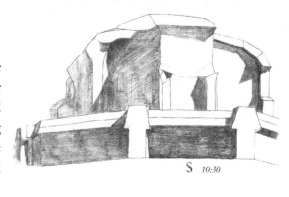

S   10:30

From the three-dimensional pillar, a cornice-like strip of molding angles up, bends horizontal, then twists flat and outward to the wings (5 and 6 in diagram). This double curve of the plane is polar to the double curve of the roofline on the front side of the three-dimensional pillar (2 and 3 in diagram). Rudolf Steiner speaks of the effect of the double curve form: "The life of the surface and the soul of the form we find by not resting content with a single curvature of a surface, but by curving the already bent plane a second time so that a double curvature results. In this way, we can cause the form to speak, and we begin to notice that deep down in our subconsciousness the analytical sense is confronted by a synthesizing sense."[14]

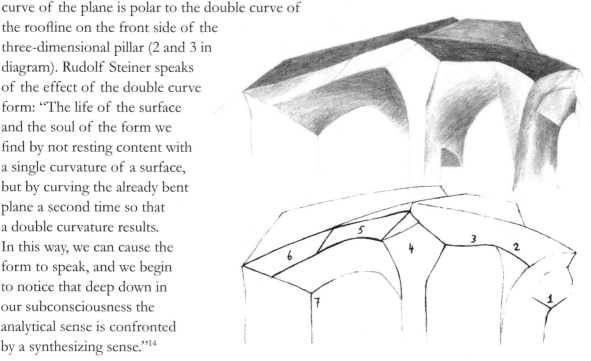

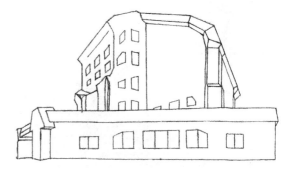

The roofline molding of the auditorium's back half compares very differently to the molding of the cornice under the roof of the stage part of the building. This difference is expressive of the very different forces at work in the meeting of load and lift in the auditorium versus the stage part of the building: an expansive double-curved form that unites horizontally with the wing, versus an angled, straight, lifting form that meets perpendicularly with the wing.

### A Sequence of Six—the Stage

Meeting the evolving quality of the number seven of the auditorium, perfect balance may be found in the number six of the stage. In the model for the building (drawing, page 135), the rear corners of the stage part were beveled; likewise, the conjoining of wall and roof were beveled. The Solothurn Canton building administration was unhappy with the planned building due to its extreme lopsidedness in its front-back difference, as they appraised it, and requested Rudolf Steiner to elaborate the stage part. He responded with the polar opposite of cropped edges: cornice molding and pilaster, or relief pillar.

The roof cornice is tripartite (upper 1, 2, 3 in drawing). Its angled slant decreases as it rises from the vertical to the horizontal. Its form thins, tapers, and lengthens as extension and expression of the change of length and angle of the roofline. The pilaster (lower 1, 2, 3 in drawing) along the rear vertical edge of the building is partitioned in two parts designating the two upper levels of the building. The terrace may be considered as an initial part of the pillar's stepped form.

Although similar in form, the difference of the cornice's angled bend and the pilaster's step expresses the sharp contrast to the polar dissimilarity of lift of wall and load of roof. The horizontal step balances the vertical aspect of the lift in the pillar's forces that buttress and break the load of the roof. The angles of the cornice express the force of the roof's load as it falls toward the rear from horizontal to vertical. These forms express the interaction of lift and load uniquely in the stage part of the building.

In the second Goetheanum, the two times three parts of cornice and pillar present a simple picture of the number six—in the perfect union of lift and load.

# 7

## *The World Soul on the World Cross*

Plato in the *Timaeus* tells of the world soul stretched on the cross of the world body. The ground plan of the great cathedrals is a picture of the world cross of the body of the earth, Christ's body. The world soul, Plato's Anima mundi, is the living being of the world, the divine element in the world, the Logos.

The anthroposophical understanding of the body of the world is four-fold consisting of the physical, etheric (life), astral (soul), and I bodies. Rudolf Steiner describes the world bodies relating to one another as currents: from the north the physical current and from the south the etheric current interweave and form the world.

In the human being, the four bodies of the physical, etheric, astral, and I relate to one another as directional currents interweaving and forming the human organism. From the human being's left flows the physical current, from the right flows the etheric current, from below flows the astral current, and from above flows the I current.[15]

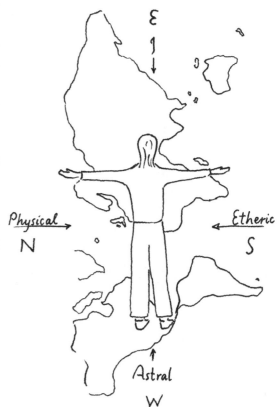

In the ground plan of the cross, the world directional currents relate to the individual currents of the human being standing facing east (or lying face down). East, the sun rises to a radiant blue sky day; west, the night descends with its brilliant stars; the left arm extends north where the land masses of the world predominate; the right arm extends south where the oceans of the world predominate.

This picture relates to the Goetheanum in the building's profile as world cross, horizontal in its relationship to the earth presenting the polar idea of the building's ground plan.

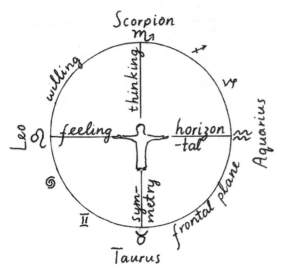

*After a blackboard
drawing (modified)
by Rudolf Steiner
9 October 1921*

The building itself in its vertical structure and frontal view presents the world in its soul aspect of the three dimensions of space: frontal, horizontal, and symmetrical. The anthroposophical understanding of the soul of the human being and of the world is three-fold consisting of thinking, feeling, and willing. In the human being, these correspond to the three planes of symmetrical, horizontal, and frontal planes of the body. The human being projects these into the cosmos dividing the stars of the zodiac through these planes.[16] This picture relates to the building's frontal view as world soul, vertical in its relationship to the starry sphere.

The building that rises on its ground plan may be viewed as the spiritual identity and properties of the three *dimensions* of space on the four *directions* of space.

The three soul forces of thinking, feeling, and willing are placed on the four currents of the bodies: physical, etheric, astral, and the I. The three soul members mediate the spaces between the four bodies, and the four bodies interplay creating a space for the soul. Into this dynamic, the human spirit enters.

From the perspective of these general considerations: in the building's division of spaces for the ground plan, the will relates the I to the astral; in the vertical levels, the feeling relates the astral to the etheric; in the building's symmetry, the thinking relates the etheric to the physical.

In the frontal view of the Goetheanum, the three planes are placed in a particular relationship. The width establishes a ground upon which to build: the feeling. This horizontal plane of the building's levels is the base upon which the drama plays out of the frontal and symmetry planes. The wide expanse of the wings unifies the frontal plane's three receding apertures. On the one hand, the frontal plane provides the connection to the unity of the background: the heights. On the other hand, the frontal plane presses forward in the gradual concentration of space: winning space in creating it: the depths. The symmetry plane of the vertical midline brings focus, orientation, and unity.

In the language of the world soul: through the warmth of feeling that is developed through interest between people, the willed intention of an idea can incarnate. The building proclaims its hope.

48

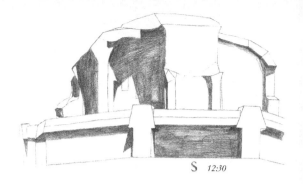

# 8

## The Goetheanum Constellation

Fourteen companion (adjacent, or ancillary) buildings designed by Rudolf Steiner surround the Goetheanum. Including the Goetheanum, the tally of the ensemble is fifteen. That is, two times seven buildings plus a fifteenth stand on the greater Goetheanum hill. Three of the buildings, the three Eurythmy Houses, constitute a single unit. So counted, twelve companion buildings circle the Goetheanum, six to the north of its east-west axis and six to the south. Rudolf Steiner considered it a necessary requirement to place around the Goetheanum such buildings designed in relationship to it. To walk the Goetheanum hill is to be in a dynamic, spatial force field of changing relationships to these buildings.

At least four characteristics add together to create a constellation through which to pass to the Goetheanum: 1) The critical placement of the buildings taking into account the contour and characteristics of the land on which they stand; 2) Their relation to the Goetheanum and to each other in distance and form may be called the social aspect of their architecture; 3) Their individually unique design may be called spiritual functionalism. 4) Their axial alignment, or placement, expresses the person who lived there or the activity engaged in for which a building was used. These four aspects interrelate into a whole. The constellation of the Goetheanum hill is like the starry constellations, a living being with a vibrant, active, creative intent.

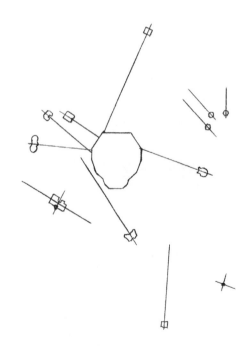

For his proposed design of residential housing, Rudolf Steiner phrased it thus, "If you know how many rooms are required and what purpose they are to serve, how many types of vertical communication there are to be, as well as what orientation and outlook the client requires, and if you also know the exact site and how the building is to relate to the Goetheanum, to the north or to the south of it, then I would claim it is possible to find an appropriate architectural solution."[17] As to their social aspect, it would be "impossible for the faintest trace of mutual incompatibility, unfriendly word or even wry glance—discontent will give way to contented smiles at these sociable and peaceful forms."[18] If receptive to their stimulus, "such buildings would be 'lawgivers' teaching love."[19]

1

Each of the fourteen companion buildings is a starry gem for the study of architecture. To lift the lid on this gem box for a moment, a few facets of this new architecture are briefly detailed.

1. The entrance steps and door to the buildings are revealing. The *Duldeck House* (1 on map, page 8) west of the Goetheanum relates to the open side of the Goetheanum with entrances on all four of its sides.

2

2. In contrast, the *Schuurman House* east of the Goetheanum relates to the closed side of the Goetheanum with a single entrance. Both buildings were designed for residential use, the first for a dentist and the second for a musician—a surprising contrast of profession and design, curved and straight forms.

3. The *Halde* northwest of the Goetheanum has dynamic steps to its entrances. The rise in elevation of steps is an exact picture of the rise in consciousness called for in entering a given space. The steps herald not only the kind of space entered but also the terrain of its placement. The Halde was built for eurythmy on land raised on a steep incline. The north entrance to the Halde (unfortunately permanently locked—drawing) has a dynamic, elaborate, sculpted stairway in polar contrast to the square cut stairs that lead to the south entrance.

3

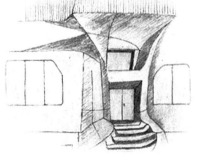

4. The *Publishing House*, a late addition in 1924 to the north side of the Goetheanum, was built to store the books of the Anthroposophical Press. The entrance is framed with two vertical, narrow windows on either side and a slightly wider window above it for what otherwise is a closed building. The door is set deep in this bunker-like building; the diminutive size of the building also emphasizes its hidden, contracted role. The roof, however, is beautifully faceted and contains the main

light source via a large skylight. The spiritual functionalism of a book stored for later use is made manifest.

5. So, too, across the road in the *Heating House* (or *Boiler Building*), the spiritual functionalism of heat combustion is revealed in the threefold upward thrust of the chimney.

6. The *Glass House* completes this northerly trio (drawing below). It was the first building Rudolf Steiner designed that was built on the hill and stands solid, squarely facing the Goetheanum. Technical details characterize it. The unusual cut of the shingles better directs the flow of rain runoff. The door handle must be pulled out while pushing the door in to enter. This counter movement to enter the building requires one to be awake—if inattentive, one's hand may get pinched in the door handle. The door (drawing right) divides the two domes with their windows. The windows, of which this building predominately consists, are sized to match those of the first Goetheanum. In the Glass House, the windows for the first Goetheanum were engraved. The Glass House divides in a non self-sufficient way what is united in the Goetheanum.

S    *13:00*

7. Due south of the Goetheanum's double space profile is *de Jaager House*, a memorial to a sculptor and residence for his widow. It is a fine example of the ancillary buildings built on the double space idea of polarity. The

51

memorial is announced with an entrance in an otherwise blank wall. A long narrow corridor leads to a spacious hallway where a large staircase climbs to a halfway landing at the back of the building, the residential part. A large window on the landing lights the space—a polar form to the façade. The landing allows for a 180° turn of the stairs, which divide left and right to the second level. From inside and on the second level, the memorial part of the building is faced: again, a wall with a door. The door opens to the atelier showcasing the artist's work. The atelier is closed to the world lit only from a skylight. In a dynamic process, the ground plan of the building is traversed joining the memorial space to the residential space, retraced on the second level to end at the atelier's exhibition space.

8–10. The three *Eurythmy Houses* further up the road are all three essentially the same in design although positioned differently to face the turn of the road. They follow in descending levels the road's turn toward the Goetheanum. This invitational turn toward the Goetheanum in a descending three-step dance can be felt to require the ensemble trio of what otherwise, if a single unit, would be an exposed and awkward standing building.

11. The *Bloomenstein House,* west of the Goetheanum on Herzental Strasse, is singularly curious in its asymmetrical front that faces not the road but the Felsli up the hill. To the left of the entrance is a bay window and to the right is a flat window. The path from the street leads up past the bay window to the entrance steps. A stairwell continues in the house on the right side imposing the external, internal asymmetry in its sagittal axis.

12–13. Not only the inner quality of the function, the relation of the parts to the whole, and the nature of the land play into the forming of an architecture that has its source in the human being, but also the person. The very biography of the person is imbedded in such building. To pass *Vreede House* on Auf der Höhe in Arlesheim on the other side of the Schwinbächli Creek divide is to know the person who lived there in their relation to the Goetheanum. With its axis not in line with the Goetheanum, it has a freer relation than the others to the building. It is halfway to the *Wegman House*, which with its clinic is in its own constellation.

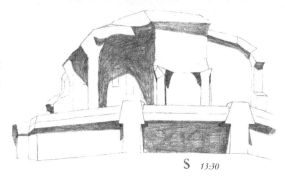

S  13:30

14. Finally, the small *Transformer Building* (drawing below) at the juncture to Rüttiweg makes conscious in form the abrupt change in the conversion of electrical current. A high voltage (used to transport the electrical current over a long stretch) is stepped down to a lower voltage (for use in house holds) and dispersed through overhead wires in cardinal directions. Two opposite, connected coils achieve the transformation.

These fourteen buildings provide a rich study for residential dwellings, utility structures, annexes, and modular housing.

The Goetheanum hill constellation creates a house for a human constellation. The Goetheanum forms awaken consciousness of karma, the hunger to address and redress the self who has its essence in biography. Each unique and exclusive life can find its identity only in inclusive participation with the other lives that belong to it. Sense perception of the spirit-moving forms of the Goetheanum may move the spirit in the beholder to open the possibility to participate in the unfolding biography in greater accord with reality.

The intent of this constellation of buildings is to create a prototype space for an encounter of human beings. This space promotes the encounter with the Goetheanum "in looking up to the Goetheanum" as Rudolf Steiner phrased it. This reverence for the spirit can lead to the experience of being seen by the Goetheanum due to its living, metamorphic quality of being.

The witnessing quality of the architecture of the Goetheanum hill promotes the capacity of freedom to meet the self in the world. This peripheral self is common to all in that it flows from the world, yet it is unique to each in the particulars of the individual life. The unforeseen occurrences, encounters, and opportunities that continually unfold present themselves to the person from outside. The conscious self is the reflection point for this life that continually streams toward one. For this life to manifest, the moment of freedom must be met with affirmation. We are continually invited to become who we are. The map of the Goetheanum hill may become a reference for the journey toward one's own spiritual biography. Where on the hill and when something occurs, may be read like sign posts. The building offers the gradual awakening to the dynamics of the intentional subtext of life.

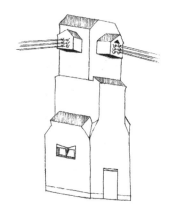

# The Temple
# Is the Human Being

### The Idea
### of the Goetheanum's Architecture

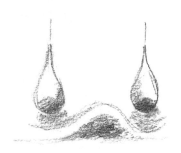

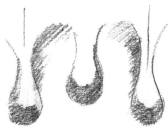

*Drawing of the pillar base motifs*
*in the large cupola of the first*
*Goetheanum—a metamorphic sequence*

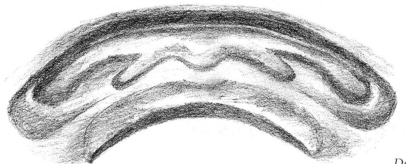

*Drawing of the second*
*building motif for the*
*first Goetheanum*

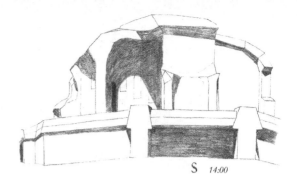

## 9

## *Architecture as Expression of the Human Physical Body*

### *The Human Being Is the Measure*

Rudolf Steiner speaks of architecture as a projection in space of the lawfulness of the human physical body.[20] In *The Temple of Man,* R. A. Schwaller de Lubicz shows the ground plan of the temple at Luxor dedicated to the spiritual conception of the human form. The Pharaonic Temple's proportions correspond with the human form's proportions. The proportions of the human form start with the feet at the entrance and continue on to the head at the inner sanctum.

Rudolf Steiner: "The proportional measures of the human form are the transitions from the etheric body to the physical body."[21] The proportional relationships of the human form reveal the life forces active within it. Sacred architecture measures space relating the human being to the forces that shape the human form.

Measurement has its origin in the dimensions of the human form. In ancient Egypt and Mesopotamia, the standard of measure was inscribed on the king's staff, of a black granite rod, and kept in the temple. This rod was the ruler that determined the measurement of the land. After the yearly flooding of the Nile River, the priests took the royal measure to re-survey the fertile fields. The basic unit of measure was the *cubit*, the oldest human measure. It measures the length from the elbow to the middle fingertip. The royal cubit (20.62 inches) subdivided into 7 *palms* (hand width) of 4 *digits* each. Later in Europe, the measure was called an *ell*, from *ulna*, the bone of the forearm. King Edward I of England required every town to have an ell-wand, sometimes attached to a corner of the market square.

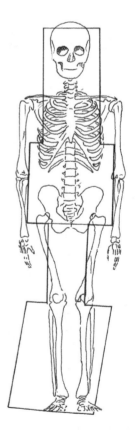

*After a drawing by*
*R. A. Schwaller de Lubicz*

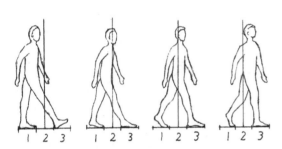

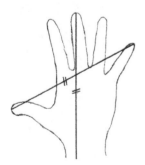

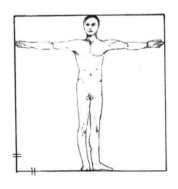

The Greeks used the *digit* (finger) as their base measure. The Romans used the *foot* as their base measure, which developed into the use of the *pace* from marching. The pace was a double stride, the right foot's swing from behind to in front of the left foot (a measure of 5 feet). One thousand paces equaled a *mile*.

*Inch* and *ounce* derive from the same word and refer to one twelfth part, the thumb's width measured at the base of the nail. Subdivisions of ½, ⅓, ¼, ⅙ divide uniquely well into twelve.

A *span* is the outstretched thumb to little finger, which is also equal to the length from the wrist to the fingertip, i.e., the outstretched hand has equal dimensions in width and length.

A *fathom* is the horizontally outstretched embracing arms, which is also equal to the height of a person, i.e., the human form's height and width of outstretched arms have equal dimensions.

The *yard* is the human stride of three feet. The yard is also midline of the chest to fingertip, or simply the entire arm. Thus, arm and leg find their relationship between form and movement.

These measurements taken from the human form and movement place the human being in relationship to the earth. However, the provincialization of measurement in the eighteenth century helped spur the search for a measurement taken from the world. Initially, the length for the *meter* (using a decimal positional system developed in the early seventeenth century) was put forward as one minute of the Earth's arc; later, as the length of a pendulum that beats at the rate of one second; then, the length of one ten-millionth of the distance between pole and equator; finally, the standard of measure was transferred outside the world and has become the distance light travels in a vacuum in a set time. This measurement decoupled the human being from the human being's activity and objectified the world by disenfranchising the human being.

In this development toward an independent and objective relationship to measurement—albeit losing the human connection to it—the architectural impulse of the Goetheanum seeks to renew the connection between architecture and the human form. Such a connection coupled with an independent outlook toward the world may provide for an individual architecture taking its source from the human being.

## The Body in Space

The Three Planes of Space—symmetrical, horizontal, and frontal—are a projection of the three planes that bisect the human form at right angles.[22] The human form through the three planes that bisect it creates space. The three planes integrate the human being with the world. The human being places him or herself in the world through this orientation.

The human form is the origin of such a qualitative differentiation of space. How space is manipulated is the art of architecture. The warehouse architecture that has blanketed and blighted the modern landscape is dyslexia of architecture that engenders an illiterate relation to the planes of space.

The planes of space have their lawful effect on the creation of form. The polarity of concave and convex, the principle of lift and load, and the inversion of left and right unite to form an outer structure for an internal space.

Rudolf Steiner's few sketches for the buildings he designed showed at times three views: front, profile, and ground plan. This characteristic need for three views to integrate a spatial form qualitatively differentiates it.

In *Goethe the Scientist*, Rudolf Steiner develops a Goethean concept of space. Space is experienced as *separation* of things, of things next to one another with distance between them. The first dimension of space relates the perceived *concrete* things to one another. In the second dimension, the initial concrete relationships are themselves related and in so doing their *abstract* ideal element sought. The third dimension relates the abstract relationships as a *unity*. Space is the idea of experiencing the world as a unity, a qualitative differentiated whole.

*The Symmetry (Sagittal) Plane* pervades nature as an imaginary line (the place of transition from a left to a right is infinitesimal). It is the quality of similar parts that inverted, mirror each other, or like a glove turned inside out, matches its mate. Such inversion and reflection is a process of thinking.

The functions of the two mirroring sides are different complementing each other and requiring integration. For example, our two eyes allow stereoscopic vision—depth perception, gauging distance, and focusing. Rudolf Steiner points out that in the human being the left eye observes objects

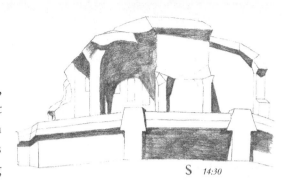

S   *14:30*

59

while the right eye senses the sensing, synthesizing the discrete observations of the left eye.[23]

The view of the symmetry line of the Goetheanum is separately placed: the allée leading to the rondel. From the rondel, one sees the building in the perfect harmony of its planes. The rondel is the place from where best to contemplate the building thinking its perfect presence before entering it.

*The Horizontal (Transverse) Plane* unites an above and below. The horizontal midline through the human being may be variously placed. A primary division is the head from the rest of the body. The arms stretched out express this division. In the horizontal plane, the hands express the human being's free potential in countless activities.

The horizontal plane projects into space the division of the Goetheanum into its three levels. This differentiation provides the harmony of the building's stature whether in viewing it from outside or climbing the stairs inside.

*The Frontal Plane* creates through a front and behind the depth axis in the human being.

The axis line of a building is the way through the building. Walking under a dome, the way ends at its center; walking down an aisle or nave, the line of perspective compels one on to pass through such a passage-like space. The Goetheanum expresses uniquely the progression through dome and aisle.

The way through the Goetheanum is met initially at its west entrance. However, to view the building in its symmetry requires one to walk down the allée away from the building countering any tendency of compulsion in the frontal plane. From the distance of the rondel, the symmetry of the building is experienced in perfect harmony with the other planes. Then the path of the depth dimension of the allée is walked in a progressive transformation of the building's vertical and horizontal planes. Entering the auditorium, the isosceles trapezoid's line of perspective to the stage widens to counter the narrowing of perspective—creating a dynamic progression that both restrains and directs one forward.

The human being experiences verticality as the complex working of the three planes. Through a front/back, the intent of the will is promoted in the vertical. As the human form is made for movement, standing is simply movement retracted to a minimum, the will to stand leading over into the will to walk. Through an above/below of uprightness, the hands may be engaged freely for life's pursuits. Through a left/right, one's uprightness is reflected in consciousness. In standing, all three planes are continually engaged.

S  *15:00*

## Two-Fold Human Being

The human physical body of bones, muscles, and nerves function to orientate the human being's form, movement, and perception in the three dimensions of space. Polarity may be found constituted in these attributes of the physical body. The rounded bones of the skull form a polarity to the radial bones of the limbs. The flexor muscles in the front of the body for bending act as a polarity to the extensor muscles in the rear of the body for stretching. The nerves for the sense organs that perceive the world serve as a polarity to the nerves that perceive the processes of will, the movements of the limbs.

The two-fold nature of head and limbs mirror each other through reincarnation. Rudolf Steiner speaks of how the limbs become the head in the subsequent incarnation.[24] The movements of the limbs along with the moral motive of action have a direct bearing on the quality of the forces of the head, its form but also the intangible qualities of speech and thought in the following incarnation.

## Reincarnation

Rudolf Steiner laid out a grand vision for metamorphic architecture as a way of schooling perception for the vision of karma. Through perceiving the metamorphic forms of the Goetheanum imaginatively, the connections may be awakened between the present life and its antecedent. Imaginative perception of the metamorphic forms in space may awaken in the beholder perception of the metamorphic forms in time of the beholder's lives. The sensitivity for the metamorphic connections of forms awakens sensitivity for the metamorphic connections of past lives.[25]

The metamorphic principle of the inside sculptural aspect of the first building may be seen in the metamorphic principle of the outside architectural aspect of the second building. The forms of the outside of the second building may school the perceiver in the law of metamorphosis of karma in one's own past lives. Such an orientation and mood toward reincarnation may transform the potential human encounters within the building.

The wisdom of the human being is the impulse for the architecture of the Goetheanum. Concurrently in Weimar, Germany, there developed what became known as organic architecture.

*Organic Architecture* received its voice from Frank Lloyd Wright, who coined the term in 1908. Along with Antonio Gaudi and others inspired by their vision, an individual, distinctive architecture arose that sought to emulate nature. Louis Sullivan in 1896 distilled the law "form follows function" from observation of nature. The life of nature is recognizable in its expression—so also architecture. An integrated building design should grow as nature grows from the inside out creating a living skin, not a dead shell. A sensibility for place and time gave context and orientation to such architecture.

Johann Wolfgang von Goethe anticipated this development developing a concept of the organic. Through participatory observation, seeing intrinsically with the seen, he formulated a way of seeing such that the whole is perceived in the relationships of the phenomena. Such seeing is a perceiving that thinks, a thinking that perceives. The idea of the organism imbues the organism such that the whole is in every part. The part exists in context of the whole as a multiplicity in unity. The separate parts are united in the movement of a dynamic form. The sequence of forms is the metamorphosis of the organizing idea intrinsic in the phenomenon's wholeness.[26]

The architectural impulse that Rudolf Steiner developed with the Goetheanum takes its start from the human being. It places the principle of metamorphosis foremost with its evolutionary sequence of becoming in the human being and in the human being's role in the nature of thinking and in the thinking of nature. The heart of metamorphosis is the principle of polarity.

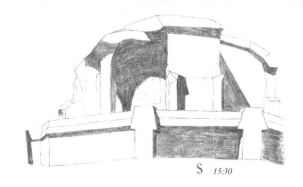

# 10

## *Polarity in Metamorphosis*

*Polarity* is the prime, original phenomenon for the idea of *metamorphosis* as developed by Johann Wolfgang von Goethe (1749–1832). Parallel to Goethe's development in Germany of the idea of metamorphosis, Samuel Taylor Coleridge (1772–1834) in England was developing a profound philosophy of polarity. Coleridge's philosophy of *polar logic* complements Goethe's applied observation of nature.

In Coleridge's writings and projected writings, his *Logosophia,* he sketched an organic structure of logic in the law of polarity: "Every power in nature and in spirit must evolve an opposite as the sole means and condition of its manifestation: and all opposition is a tendency to re-union. The law of polarity is the manifestation of one power by opposite forces. Polarity is not a mere balance, but a generative interpenetration."[27] Opposites are contradictory and exclusionary to one another, polarity is not; it is inclusionary confirming distinctions without division.

Contemporaneously, Johann Gottlieb Fichte (1732–1814) and Georg Wilhelm Friedrich Hegel (1770–1831) elaborated an organic idealistic dialectics. Dialectics *(through + logos),* the art of thinking developed by the ancient Greeks, received a new impulse in their hands. Hegel's dialectic method proceeds in a movement of concepts that germinate out of one another. A relationship of concepts to each other is developed to reveal what is more in each. Beginning the organic edifice of sequential categories is *Being (Sein)* deriving *Nothing (Nicht-Sein)* from it and resolving both in *Becoming (Werden),* each step proceeding with the resistance of an opposite force.[28]

The resistance of overcoming leads to increased perfection. William Blake observed that "without contraries there is no progression;" and Rudolf Steiner: "No development is possible unless contradiction lay in the very nature of things."[29]

For Hegel, identity is only possible through its relation to non-identity. Identity implies an internal difference; differences constitute identity. Negation, or nothing, is not external to things but internal and inherent. The *Absolute* must pass through its *Nothing* to its completion in the *Concrete*. The negative phase is overcome through *sublation*, the integral transcendence of opposites. Only the whole is true. The final identity of *self* is constituted by the difference between an *I* and *not-I*. Being free is possible only through others' freedom, and freedom is only possible in selfless love.

The triadic structures used by Fichte and Hegel are condensed, if simplified, in *Thesis-Antithesis-Synthesis*. The German philosopher Heinrich Moritz Chalybäus (1796–1862) promulgated this formulation to characterize Hegelian dialectic (although Hegel never used it).

Coleridge describes this triune relation thus: "Identity of thesis and antithesis is the substance of all being; their opposition the condition of all manifest existence; and every phenomenon is the exponent of a synthesis as long as the opposite energies are retained in that synthesis."[30] Synthetic thought relates the analytical separate elements; it develops out of itself and out of nature with which it is congruent.

The key premise to organic thinking and of these thinkers is the convergence of thinking with nature. Thinking is sovereign of both the subject mind and object nature. The act of thinking is the ground of being, of the world, the Logos, and of the unity of self-consciousness. Polarity knows the one through the other and requires for each the existence of both. Coleridge: "The essential duality of Nature arises out of its productive unity. All life consists of the strife of opposites to unite, an individuation that presupposes the whole."[31]

In *The Philosophy of Freedom*, Rudolf Steiner points to the polarity of *observation* and *thinking* as the primary antithesis, "The two fundamental pillars of our spirit." It is due to the "two-fold nature of our being" that reality appears at first as a dyad. "The act of knowing overcomes this twoness (Zweiheit) by fusing the two elements of reality, the percept and the concept gained by thinking, into a complete thing."[32]

To Coleridge's primal law of polarity and Hegel's triune being, Goethe developed an exact science of the metamorphosis of plants. Goethe's ideal perception of the archetypal plant is an alternating contraction and expansion of the spatial growth of the plant. Its metamorphoses develop intensively with each extensive stage integrated in the next. The generative plane of the leaf unfolds the myriad plant forms in a sequence of temporal transformations of the sap becoming rarefied.

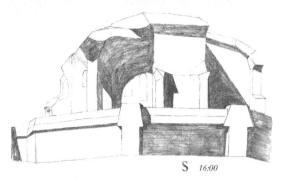
S   16:00

Stage 1: The contracted seed's unique warmth space yields receptively to the creative forces from the cosmos.

Stage 2: The cosmic forces engage with the earthly elements and the shoot breaks the surface of the earth and expands. The darkness draws forth the root; the sunlight draws out the leaf with its buoyant surface tension in myriad forms.

Stage 3: The calyx brings the linear stem and planar branching of leaves to a halt contracting to the point of a bud.

Stage 4: The hub breaks open to expand to the perimeter of the sphere in radial petals. The generation of the corolla's space is the individuality of color.

Stage 5: The forces of the spherical dynamics of color concentrate in the center of the sphere; the dynamics of polar opposition are seen in the reproductive organs of stamen and pistil that produce in synthesis a new creation. A pollen grain's two cells provide double fertilization to the seed's ovule and endosperm; the endosperm, placenta-like, provides nourishment to the ovule (embryo).

Stage 6: The fruit (ovary) is the expanded new resultant in which lies the new seed (ovule).

This rhythmic and qualitative sequence of six through comparative relationships between the stages reveals a plant's uniqueness. For example, plants whose flowers grow below their leaf development close to the ground may have fragrant roots, such as Wild Ginger (*Asarum candensis*) or Wild Sarsaparilla (*Aralia nudicaulis*). That is, the root of the plant takes on the flower qualities of fragrance in relation to the flower's position.

The flower takes the expansive middle placement in the sequence of Goethe's archetypal plant. The flower expresses

Wild Sarsaparilla

Wild Ginger

65

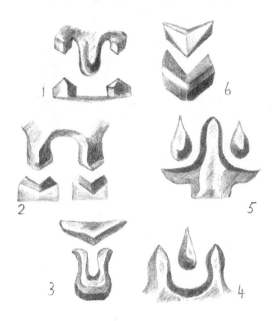

*Drawings of the capital motifs from the small (above) and large (below) domes of the first Goetheanum: arranged to reveal the polar symmetry principle.*

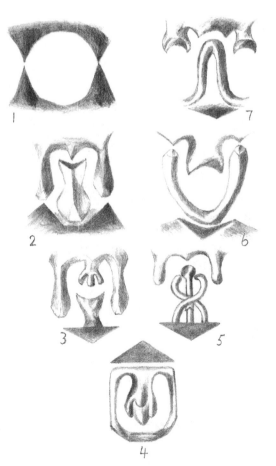

the identity, the signature of the plant and is its freer, centrally placed element. The plant takes in the lawful starry world (seed) to discover its own identity (flower) out of which to create its own creation (fruit). The leaf is the protean element through these metamorphoses: the plant is wholly leaf.

Rudolf Steiner's seminal thinking in the early days of the development of anthroposophical thought rests squarely on the singular achievements of Goethe. Steiner incorporated and developed the idea of polarity in an all-encompassing and far-reaching way. To Goethe's sequential development of an organism out of polarity, Steiner discovered a polar counter-stream from the future. Thus, the beginning and end of an organic sequence are polar to one another. The second stage is polar to the second to last, and so on. These are streaming forces in which, like integral numbers, the dips and crests of the waves are highlighted.

Rudolf Steiner describes this process for the capitals of the large dome in the first Goetheanum: "When the raised embossed forms of the first capital are turned inside out, inverted, then forms are produced that fill out exactly the engraved depressions of the seventh seal. The same occurs for the second and sixth capitals, third and fifth capitals and the fourth stands for itself in the middle."[33] Or again two years later: "I was surprised to find as I arrived at the seventh capital how the raised forms of the first capital were inverted like a glove turned inside out, not geometrically but artistically, exactly fitting into the depressions of the last capital. The same was the case with the second and sixth capital and with the third and fifth, and the fourth stood in the middle."[34]

Similarly with the written word, to create continuity of thought in writing, Rudolf Steiner suggests such an approach: "To write with style one ought already to have the last sentence within the first, and while writing the second sentence have in mind the last but one. One should have the whole essay before one when one writes."[35]

The polarities that thus arise are of different kinds and create together a matrix of forces. To the development out of polarity (Goethe) is added the symmetry principle in the counterstream (Steiner). Together in their meeting they create the polar oppositions in which nature holds itself.

The American transcendentalist philosopher, Ralph Waldo Emerson, described this great polarity in his essay *Compensation* thus: "Polarity, or action and reaction, we meet in every part of nature; in darkness and light; in heat and cold; in the ebb and flow of waters; in male and female; in the systole and diastole of the heart; in the centrifugal and centripetal gravity. If the south attracts, the north repels. To empty here, you must condense there. The value of the universe contrives to throw itself into every point. If the good is there, so is the evil; if the affinity, so the repulsion; if the force, so the limitation. Thus is the universe alive. All things are moral. That soul which within us is a sentiment, outside of us is a law."

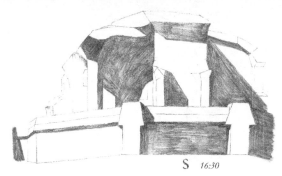

S   *16:30*

Synthesis out of polarity Rudolf Steiner describes as a trinity: "All life depends upon the activity and the interworking of primordial trinities: a unifying, a differentiation, a rhythmic intermediate condition [...] the spiritual and physical are present as a polarity with a rhythmic interweaving of the two as the third or the three-in-the-one, one-in-the-three."[36] Two is the number of physical manifestation; three is the number of the spirit.[37] The principle of polarity pierces, breaks through, and transcends the physical with the spirit into a creative new whole.

The sequencing, opposing, mirroring (or inversion), and number principle of polarity constitute the principle of metamorphosis. Discrete parts assume their cohesive whole, creation evolves its sequential life, and the human being finds a self-creative spiritual potential through this principle.

Rudolf Steiner's architecture may be explored in the relations and movements of polarities. For the prototype form for the design of the Duldeck House, Steiner gave the simple image of a bean with its characteristic concave, convex form. The realized symphonic majesty of the first Goetheanum contained the entre evolution of the human being.

## *Polarity as the Building Idea*
The ground plan blueprint idea for the second Goetheanum is the polar conjoining of an auditorium space with a stage space. The auditorium was given an isosceles trapezoid form and the stage a rectangular, almost square form. The interpenetration of this polar space requires each space to metamorphose into the other.

*After a sketch by Rudolf Steiner*

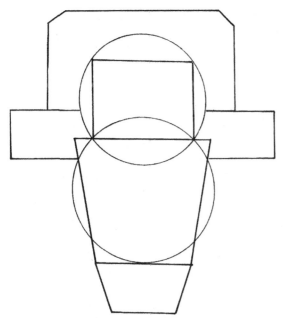

*After a sketch by Rudolf Steiner*

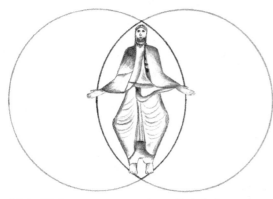

*Vesica Piscis*          *Autun Cathedral—tympanum*

Rudolf Steiner sketched the ground plans for both the first and second buildings employing the elements of cross and circle. A 1913 sketch shows a cross form extending inside the two cupola circles. The cross form, modified, became the ground plan for the second Goetheanum around the two circles of the cupolas. The interlocking circles unite polarities. The cross divides head from body in the joining of vertical and horizontal.

Rudolf Steiner's initial presentation of the idea of the first Goetheanum to Alexander Strakosch in 1911—as later the same year to Carl Schmid-Curtius—was simply, "Take two circles that reciprocally interpenetrate one another."[38] "The difference in size," Rudolf Steiner later explained, "Simply signifies that in the large cupola the physical aspect is paramount, while in the smaller one we have tried to make the spiritual aspect predominant."[39] The union of physical with spiritual is the unique free place of the human being.

The vesica piscis is such a form. It is formed by two circles the same size the perimeters of which intersect each other's center. In the portals of the great cathedrals of Europe, the Christ is often portrayed framed in the space of the circles' intersection, called the mandorla. It symbolizes the coincidence of opposites, the integration of opposing worlds, the place of meeting—of birth, transformation, balance, and synthesis.

The genesis for the second building developed from its introduction during Christmas 1923 to the middle of March 1924 with the creation of the model. Initially, a rectangular auditorium with a semicircular stage was conceived. This plan changed to an isosceles trapezoid auditorium and a rectangular, almost square stage.

The choice of the isosceles trapezoid form for the auditorium is a reverse-polar form to the functional purpose of the auditorium. The purpose of the auditorium is to create a space for many to focus on one or a few. The isosceles trapezoid form counters this focus in opening outward toward the stage. It counters the tendency of compulsion of the perspective narrowing toward the stage. Its gesture is to free the perception toward the stage.

The square is a perfect form for spatial orientation on the stage. In William Shakespeare's Globe Theater, within the circle of the auditorium, the stage was square. It provides equal spatial dimensions for the performers' orientation. Its gesture is to free the inner will of the performers.

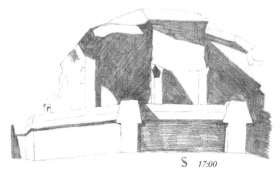

S   17:00

The outer form of the building with the gradual stepped rise of the roof from stage to auditorium must find its reflection in the internal space: the auditorium descends to the stage and the stage looks up to the auditorium. This counter movement of reverence and awe must be resolved. The meeting between the two at the curtain requires resolution in the language of polarity of the union of opposites in a whole.

The building par excellence is the great revelation of polarity. Rudolf Steiner: "Our building had to be a twofold structure. Its forms express the polar nature of the human being."[40] The relation between the human being and the architecture of the Goetheanum as well as the principle of polarity is spoken of in one breath. The polarity of our lives is addressed: of the lower self and the higher self, of the striving of the human being from the consciousness of earthly sense perception to the consciousness of cosmic spirit perception. It is the striving of Faust in Goethe's drama—the figure of Faust prominently depicted on the small cupola of the first Goetheanum.

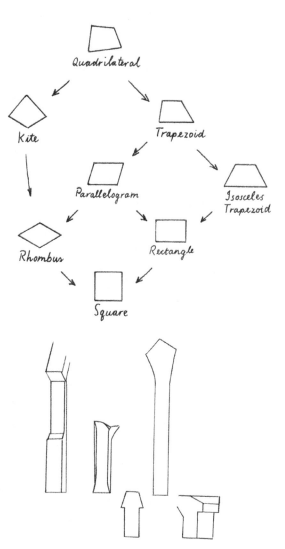

Rudolf Steiner describes the polar interpenetration of mirroring principles that was achieved in the first Goetheanum: "The interpenetration of the two domes expresses the inner connection of the two elements which mirror one another." For the building's quality of organic architecture, he described, "The living quality of our building is expressed in the fact that the consciousness of one dome is reflected in the other, that the two domes mirror one another." Finally, as secondary, "The further stage of the building, the artistic stage expressing as image the concepts of spiritual science, can only come into being because we have succeeded in achieving this interpenetration of the double dome motif."[41] Although these remarks were made in 1914 for the first Goetheanum, the fundamental design function did not change for the second building.

## Metamorphosis

Rudolf Steiner compared the internal forms of the first Goetheanum to a *Gugelhupftopf* or a *Napfkuchentopf,* Viennese cake molds similar to a marble cake pan (a circular pan with a circular form in the middle) or a bowl-like cake pan.[42] The cake was the experience in the soul when looking at the forms. Similar to a hat for the head, the cake pan is there for the cake, the positive substance and matter of the cake pan. The cake is metaphor for the experience of looking at the building's forms, of the impressions made by the forms. The consciousness that the forms of the building awaken is the building's purpose. Whether consciousness may awaken on the experience of these forms rests on each individual. How the consciousness awakens is the genius of the forms, which function like a "spiritual carriage" in which to progress.[43]

The key forms of the first Goetheanum were presented as sequences. The individual forms were the Gugelhupftopf. The spaces between the forms were the cake, the act in thinking relating how one form changed to the next. Metamorphosis is another word for this change and thinking is another word for relating. The cultivation of relating metamorphosis is the cultivation of thinking itself in its essential reality.

Rudolf Steiner: "In our building, it is not the surrounding walls that are of importance, it is what is enclosed within the surrounding walls. And within the walls will be the feelings and thoughts of the people who are in the building. These will develop aright if those who are in the building turn their eyes to its boundary, feel the forms and fill these forms with forms of thought. Through Spiritual Science man must learn to work his way out of the Gugelhopf mold into the Gugelhopf itself. The cake is in this case the spiritual. To enter into the world of the spirit is our endeavor."[44]

The first building's forms not only influenced the thoughts and mood, but also the speech of the beholder. What might be spoken in this space would want to be in accord with and attuned to its forms. The dynamic power of the word was to give utterance to the thoughts, reveal the riddle, and express the divinity of the human being. The spirit language of Rudolf Steiner matched, met, and manifested the metamorphic sequential movement of forms. The forms of the first building acted like a heavenly sounding board resounding like an echo, not unlike the sounding board of the human body as the house for the spoken word.[45]

*17:30*

# 11

# *Load and Lift*

With the forces of load and lift, the starting point of and prime theme in architecture is finally addressed. However, this theme though elementary is difficult to grasp in its enormity. Forms may be perceived and imagined. Load and lift must be intuited, crept into, and existentially united with.

Rudolf Steiner outlines the difficulty. "Suppose you have two posts set up like pillars. Imagine you lay a third post across the top of them. If men believe that they 'know' why the two pillars support the beam, they are under an illusion. All the concepts that exist of cohesion, adhesion, forces of attraction, and repulsion are at bottom only hypotheses on the part of external knowledge. We count upon these external hypotheses in our actions; we are convinced that the two posts supporting the beam will not give way if they are of a certain thickness. But we cannot understand the whole process which is connected with this any more than we understand the movement of our legs when we walk."[46] The human body's structure and a building's structure both have to do with the will, and the will lives in the unconscious of the human being.

The ancient Greek temple balanced load and lift in great harmony. This achievement comes historically between the load, or weight, of the ancient Egyptian pyramid and the lift, or lightness, of the medieval cathedral. The Goetheanum building impulse infuses as a new demand in the further development of working with these two forces the element of metamorphosis. Balance is sought in the sequential development of load and

71

lift. For metamorphoses, the demands of load and lift are in continual change. To discover their unfolding dynamic requires new capacities to relate with these forces if mechanical rest is to be overcome.

*Form and Structure* unite in architecture. In architecture, form speaks the language of structure. The genius of architecture is to reveal through forms the spiritual reality of the structure.

The engineer's concern with statics is the study of the forces of pressure on structures. If a form is not found to coincide with the forces concerned, then a sense for the truth of reality is lacking.

This conundrum raises the interesting dilemma of the engineering construction of the Goetheanum's two great three-dimensional pillars. These columns do not support the roof at all. Great beam structures with support trusses run internally across the width of the roof and anchor the two columns from above. Structurally, the columns hang contradicting the carrying form of the columns.

The forces at work in the geological construction of the earth, such as the pressure involved in rock faults, are analogous to the activity in architecture. Specifically, these activities sought in the forces involved in the creation of the Jura limestone hills around the Goetheanum can be distilled and transposed in the forms of the Goetheanum. The physical place receives its expressive human voice in an architecture embodying it.

The ancient Greek temple, shrine-like, related the gods to a geographical location. The features of the landscape corresponded with the features of the particular god. With the Goetheanum, the exterior architectural features relate to its surroundings. The building's design conveys its relationship to the landscape, not the statue in the shrine as in ancient Greece.

*Movement and Balance* may also be found in the structure and dynamics of the human body. The flexor muscles in the front part of the body are responsible for the body's ability to bend. The extensor muscles in the rear part of the body allow for the body's ability to stretch. Flexor and extensor control means these muscles work well together providing muscle balance. Through a precise sequence of movements in the first half-year of life, the infant achieves this balance. Raised to consciousness, these two qualities can find their activities in architecture. Rudolf Steiner used the verbs *bend* or *bow (biegen* or *beugen)* and *stretch* or *spread (ausdehnen)* to describe the activities in architecture found both in geology and in the anatomy of the human form.

S    *18:00*

The fundamental qualities of lift and stretch of which the human body is capable become projected into architecture. One is where one's weight is; the body is sensed as weight. The human being has the wonderful capacity to carry this weight effortlessly. The human being lifts in the vertical. The human being stretches in the horizontal in every stride of the leg and in every grasp of the hand for the objects of the world. These two qualities become translated into the lift and load of architecture.

Another approach to balance as the synthesis of load and lift in the conjoining of the architectural elements of wall and roof may be modeled on the balance of the human body. My experience of balance is continually changing depending on the positioning and support of my body's weight. Whether I stand balancing over the arch of my foot, on the heels, or on the toes, my experience of balance changes. Leaning slant forward over the foot's arch with a plumb line from forehead to ball of the foot, my experience of weight is the lightness of uprightness (eurythmy sound gesture of "e" [German "i"]). Leaning back on the heels with the plumb line of the forehead falling over the heels, my weight shifts back, my gaze up in an opening gesture (eurythmy sound gesture of "ah" [German "a"]). Tilting my stance forward with the plumb line of the forehead falling past the toes, my weight shifts forward, my gaze down in an enclosing gesture (eurythmy sound gesture of "o"). In standing up, I stretch and experience my weight in resistance to gravity; in sitting down, I bend and experience giving my weight to gravity. In everyday movements, but also

73

in eurythmy, which is an art of balance as well as movement, a rich field of exploration is possible concerning load and lift.

Finally, the mystery use of the two interlocking triangles of Solomon's Seal is the great example of the human body's relation to load and lift. Rudolf Steiner describes an exercise integrating these two triangles. In this exercise, the legs step apart sideways and the arms stretch up and out. The two triangles imaginarily close both at the feet and the hands from the left to the right side. These directional forces are to be experienced in the marrow of the bones concentrating on the experience of the words, "Light streams upward, Weight bears downward."[47] This exercise was practiced in the mystery centers of the past and lead to real thinking (concretely with the whole human organism) and perception of the spirit.

This imagination of the harmonious interpenetration of the human spirit with the temple of the body is an image of the Holy Grail. The task of architecture is to participate in this realization. A building's engineering proceeds from marking the foundation to erecting walls to spanning the roof. A temple's idea incarnates from above down: roof–walls–foundation.

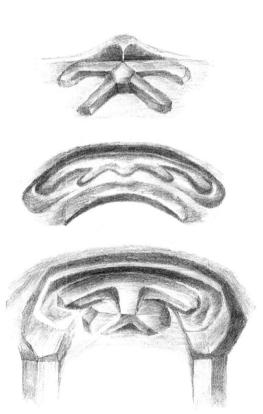

*The Building Motifs* that Rudolf Steiner gave for the first and then the second Goetheanum express in seed form the forces of lift and load worked out in the buildings. For the first Goetheanum, the motif form was prominently and massively chiseled in three metamorphic changes: outside above the west terrace entrance; inside the large cupola above the proscenium arch; and at the far end of the small cupola above the niche for the sculpture. In each case, the motif forms express the meeting of and transition to the succeeding spaces.

For the second Goetheanum, on 1 January 1924, two and a half months prior to the creation of the model for the building, Rudolf Steiner sketched on the blackboard the façade for the new building. It is a potent distilled encapsulation heralding the future building. (A drawing after Rudolf Steiner's blackboard sketch for the second Goetheanum is on the back cover. Below it is a drawing of the sketch's colors transposed to the completed building's façade—author's interpretation.)

In the sketch, the white strokes above express load. The golden-yellow pillar shape expresses lift. This polarity holds a second polarity: the lemon-yellow form that comes forward and down and the blue that recedes out and up. Nestled between these is the beginning of a pentagon chalked in pale red. Rudolf Steiner spoke of how these forms sketched on the blackboard sought to express the two qualities of invitation and protection. The load of the roof protects; the lift of the pillar receives. The meeting of these polar forms invite one in.

Although Rudolf Steiner was adamant that no pentagon form was symbolically represented in the Goetheanum, the motif forms of both the first and second buildings do indicate a form with the quality of five. This form is potently present in both buildings, but what does it reveal? The motifs may be examined in considering the structural forces of beam and arch.

The loading on a beam exerts compression forces on its upper portion, a pushing and condensing force, causing the structural movement of the beam's length to contract. On the beam's lower portion, a tensile (tension) force results, a pulling and stretching force, causing the beam's length to expand. These two forces are in equilibrium along the neutral axis, which divides the beam horizontally. The action of the load results in the beam's reaction of sagging and eventually splitting.

The arch was a major architectural innovation. The corbel arch with its offsetting successive courses of stone and with a simple capstone is an in-between step in the evolution of the arch. The true arch is a pure compression structure with no tensile force. The arch's keystone at the apex ties the curved span of stones together, yet it receives the least stress. The vertical compression forces are transferred through the curve of the adjacent wedge-shaped blocks (called voussoirs) downward to the beginning of the curve line (called springers, or footers). The curved arch rests on piers and the compression force acts as a lateral outward thrust force requiring abutments.

Rudolf Steiner's motif for the second Goetheanum depicts an enveloping force and a receptive force that combine to create the pale red trapezoidal form. The two inverse force forms find an equilibrium in this synthesis. Out of the polarity of the vertical forces of load and lift and the polarity of their interaction in the horizontal of compression and tensile forces, the building's keystone form, the isosceles trapezoid, may be seen to arise.

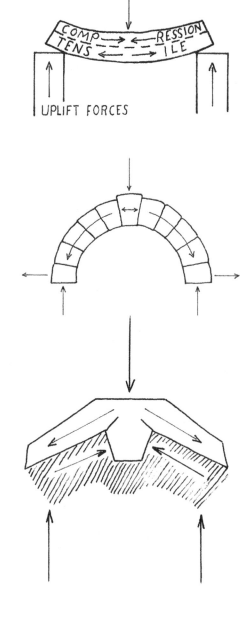

75

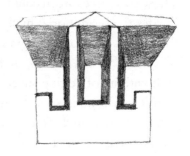

# The Inside

## House for the Word

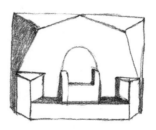

*Drawing of the pillar base
motifs in the small cupola of
the first Goetheanum*

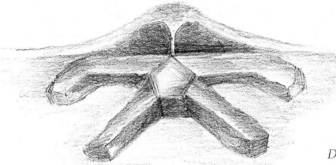

*Drawing of the third
building motif for the
first Goetheanum*

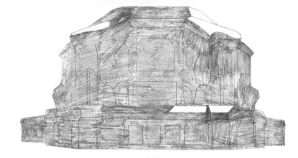

## *12*

## *Ark, Temple, and Goetheanum*

*Noah's Ark* and Solomon's Temple reveal the mystery task of architecture in humanity's evolution. Not only is the human form the source for sacred building, but conversely the building is the source for the human form. Integrated in the very becoming of the human being, architecture influences the human being in proportion and form.

Rudolf Steiner: "When man stretches his arms above him, he has the measurements of the Ark of Noah, the measurements of the present-day human body."[48] The Ark was three stories and measured 300 cubits long, 50 cubits broad, and 30 cubits high. These measures imprinted themselves upon the human being, Rudolf Steiner continues, so that after death the life body would expand to the Ark's dimensions determining in turn the length, width, and breadth of the physical body for the subsequent incarnation in our present fifth age. For this conferral, the ratio is 30 to 5 to 3. If the proportions of these numbers are considered, they accurately determine the dimensions of the human form of our age (what Steiner designates as the fifth age from 7227 BC to 7893 AD): the ratio of height with hands stretched above the head, to breadth at the shoulder, to thickness from the breastbone to the backbone.

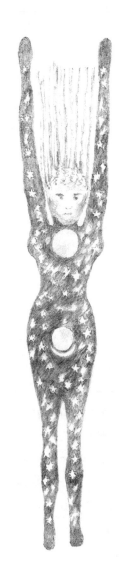

An image of such a cosmic presentation is the goddess Nut, the mother of the sky, painted on the inside lid of the Egyptian sarcophagus. Stars, sun, and moon are her body. Her hands stretch over her head. Her body bends encompassing

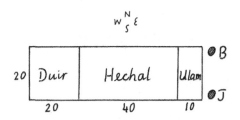

the bow of the heavens. The being of the heavens welcomed the human being after death to fill it with the soul's earthly won dimensions, the thought form of the physical prototype.

*Solomon's Temple,* as Rudolf Steiner explains developing the theme, carries hidden within its measurements the measure of the human physical form for the sixth age far in the future. Finished around 950 BC, Solomon's Temple was divided into three rooms. 1) The Ulam was the vestibule measuring 10 cubits deep, 20 cubits wide, and 30 cubits high. It may be seen to emphasize the vertical dimension of the heights and the uprightness of the human form. 2) The Hechal was the long room measuring 40 cubits deep, 20 cubits wide, and 30 cubits high. It may be seen to emphasize the horizontal dimension with the activity of the hands in relating to the three symbols of faith: the altar, the Menorah with its lights representing the seven stages of the soul's development of consciousness, and the twelve consecrated loaves of bread representing the nourishment of the spirit from out the cosmos of completion. 3) The Dvir, which faced west where the sun extinguished itself, was the Holy of Holies and measured 20 cubits deep, 20 cubits wide, and 20 cubits high. The equal measure of this cube emphasized the harmony of all three dimensions. Its darkness and its content, the Covenant, proclaimed the meeting with the presence of God. It was a picture of the perfect spiritual dimension of the human being, which is not to be realized till the light-filled, crystalline, golden cube of the New Jerusalem far in the future.

The Dvir is twice the length of the Ulam. The Dvir is half the length of the Hechal. The third room synthesizes in balance the contraction, expansion polarities of the first two rooms. The Dvir's width remains a constant, but its height is a third shorter than the other two rooms—an experience of coming to oneself. Through these dimensions, Solomon's Temple became a living place of offering and promise. They imprinted themselves for a far future when the human form will carry in its nature the idealized relationships of the free human, a place where thinking takes on the qualities of feeling, feeling takes on the qualities of willing, and willing takes on the qualities of thinking, as presented in Rudolf Steiner's poem, "Ecce Homo."

Ecce Homo
In the heart weaves feeling,
In the head shines thinking,
In the limbs strengthens willing.
Weaving shine,
Strengthening weave,
Shining strengthen:
That is the human being.

– Rudolf Steiner

*Steiner's Goetheanum* may be seen to comprise the threefold vertical levels of the Ark with the threefold horizontal partitioning of the rooms of Solomon's Temple, i.e., a 3 x 3 = 9 spaces. The vertical relation may be considered as a threefold development of the individual. The horizontal relation may be considered as a threefold development of community. The integration of the individual's spiritual path with community is then the congruence, a path through the heart, which is the potential genius of the Goetheanum.

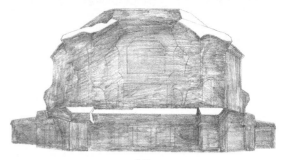

W  *11:00*

Entered from the west, the vestibule lobby is a quiet, dark, windowless, comparatively low-ceilinged, empty space that presents a mystery. A door ahead and dual stairs that sweep up left and right present the directional forms of the depth and vertical axes. In the vestibule lobby, the sense world is stilled. One stands still orientating. The space receives one inviting an encounter with oneself.

Proceeding through the doorway ahead, the second ground level space is entered. It is a cavernous space divided up with pillars. This second foyer is used for social encounters.

The third ground level space is a small theater. The size of its seating area plus stage measures the dimensions of the main stage above and was originally intended as a rehearsal space for the main stage. Between the two stages, a third space, an orchestra pit, was envisaged by Rudolf Steiner but not realized due to budget constraints.

*Drawing of a sculpture designed by Rudolf Steiner for the ground level vestibule of the first Goetheanum— a form for spatial orientation.*

Proceeding from the vestibule lobby up the open sweep of stairs, one enters upon the mystery of the vertical axis. Those who are parted with on the ground level are encountered again in the turn of the stairs on the middle level where the cross traffic from either side intermingles. The stairs spiral to partly face toward the terrace door of the middle level. In the light-filled vestibule on the second level, the inclination to pause and linger is experienced in the expansiveness over the elevation attained. A new orientation is gained: the harmony of the middle. The mystery of the building begins to reveal itself.

Rudolf Steiner describes where Jehovah breathed the magical breath of life into Adam: into the middle part of his spatial being. "There in the midst of man, bounded from left and right, above and below, before and behind, is an intervening space where the breath of Jehovah enters directly into the

physical, spatial human being. There, in the middle, Jehovah created man like a cube."[49] It is the space in the human being free from the influences of Lucifer, from above, right, and front and from Ahriman, from below, left, and behind directed toward the six surfaces of this cube. There in the heart, the human being may win free space to evolve into the cube of the New Jerusalem.

The cube may be seen as the dimension of the inside front part of the middle level. The steps from the ground external door pass through it to the upper level with its door to the main internal space of the building. The middle level corridor passes through it to the terrace. The measure of this cube is an empty space to pass through into the six directions of space pausing from one direction to another. In the horizontal plane, a pause may be enjoyed in climbing or descending the stairs. In the symmetry plane, a crossover from one side of the open space to the other may be woven in the climb of the stairs. In the frontal plane, the corridor opens out onto the terrace. To enter the cubic space from the first level, third level, or corridor is to pass from dark, narrow spaces into a light-filled space with great expanses of external views. This harmonious orientation of all six spatial directions is unique in the building and is combined with the orientation of the inside and outside of the building.

Passing outside onto the terrace, one discovers anew the building from outside. An intimate encounter with the building from outside is made possible from within the confines of a cloister-like wall and at an elevated level. The dimensions of the building are there much more at eye level, accessible and close at hand, where the forms are more revealing, dynamic, detailed, and personal. At the elevation of the terrace, its circumnavigation allows distant views across the hill and near views into the close and intimate breathing of the movement of the Goetheanum's form.

This between space of a terrace-balcony allows for an outside space to be accessed from an inside space. The experience of entering this space of the Goetheanum has a hallowed feeling of both vulnerability and commanding strength. One enters the inner aspect of the outside of the building.

In contrast, from within the building and turning away from the great, almost square window and passing along the corridor of the second level, one enters the center of the building (which will be discussed last).

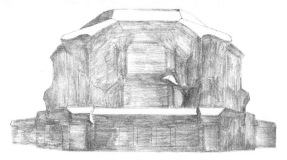

Continuing up the stairs, one reaches the vestibule third level. It provides a third orientation: the heights. The stairs join to hang a narrow bridge to the face of the towering wall and a ledge for a heavy door. Stopping and turning on these narrow stairs, one is bathed in the red glow and engraved image of the towering window with its admonition to develop the throat chakra. The window's image dominates this high perch with utter earnestness. The spirit in one's soul is met on the mountaintop and in the wilderness: the guardian of the threshold.

There is a threshold from the vertical journey in the west to the ensuing horizontal journey toward the east. From this narrow and highest elevated stand with its earnest warning, the auditorium is entered. In the auditorium, the space expands in a sweep of shimmering light and color forward, up and down, left and right. From the auditorium's backspace, the commanding vantage point of the interior is experienced due to the integration of the symmetry. It is the way for a procession. Ahead and below is the stage with its curtain of expectation.

The auditorium can also be accessed from the south entrance to the building. The auditorium itself has a south and north entrance by the stage. The path from the south entrance of the building to the auditorium is vastly different than from the west. Entering the south door to the building, one is immediately in the active area of the building. A humbler and lighter relationship to the building is found on entering this side door. The stairwell for the two-and-a-half level climb to the auditorium is single, narrow, and can be congested. Entering the auditorium from the south entrance, one experiences the internal, social character of the auditorium with its asymmetry.

It is also possible to enter the auditorium from the north side. No direct path leads there, and few take this quiet path. The north door of cathedrals was the burial door for the dead.

These seven spaces frame an eighth, the middle space of the middle level: a corridor from which eight rooms branch off. At the center of the building, this compressed space is positioned to perceive the spaces around it. It may be compared with the heart and the blood circulation. Although easily accessible, it is yet hidden. An inter-exchange with this space would reveal its character and function.

In a 1924 drawing for the design of the building (below), Rudolf Steiner drew three corridors for the second level. The center corridor that is there now he labeled *darker corridor*. Two other corridors were added running parallel to it along the outer walls of the building, which allowed them to have windows. These he labeled *lighter corridors*. Although the design for the lighter corridors was discarded in the final building plan, this design emphasizes the dynamic quality of the light and dark interplay between which color arises according to Goethe's color theory. Between the planned north and south lighter corridors and the single darker corridor in the middle is a space for color: the eight rooms. In an early plan for the room functions of the middle level, the eight rooms were designated in part as "ateliers" for the Sections of the School for Spiritual Science. Rudolf Steiner created the Sections as research departments for the various fields of culture. Section ateliers allow a space for active exchange in the different areas of human endeavor united under one roof.

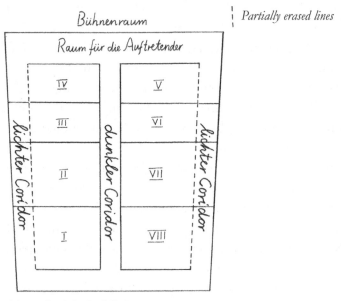

*After a sketch by Rudolf Steiner*

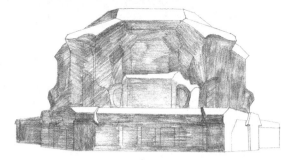

# 13

# *A Path through the Colored Windows*

Images give meaning and life to a narrative through the order of their sequence. The medieval cathedrals with their sculptures, paintings, and stained glass windows were for the illiterate people a Poor Man's Bible. The fresco murals masterfully executed by unknown artists in the obscurest of churches high up in the Alps such as in Clugen to the famous Scrovengi Chapel in Padua or the Sistine Chapel in Rome imprint their story with dynamic effect on the devout pilgrim. Iconographical programmes are cross-referenced in rich context, and skillfully placed images in opposite and parallel arrangements inform a complex biblical narrative integrated in a single scheme.

A remarkable instance of image sequences is the *Biblia Pauperum*. Far from being a "Pauper's Bible," they are illuminated manuscripts or later printed block-books from the fourteenth century. Parallel correspondences are illustrated between the Old and New Testaments juxtaposing three typologically-related images to address a theme. The changing relationship to the common theme provides a profound meditation on the structure of time. The past prefigures the future and the future fulfills the past, "For it is written."

*From the British Block-book Biblia Pauperum: Esau sells his birthright, the Temptation of Christ, and the serpent tempts Adam and Eve.*

Rudolf Steiner proposes the moral possibilities of working with such lawful sequencing: "Moral strength can be derived out of the successive sequence of two paintings, and even more so out of three. It is the working together of two motives that makes available free forces in man. If the task were to paint one painting, then one would need to proceed differently. The two motives would need to work directly together."[50]

The nine triptych colored windows of the Goetheanum are such a sequence of stations. Each triptych contains a central theme with a left and right temporal response. The side panels of the triptych are a working out in a polar dynamic the potential of the center panel. The right panel is the metamorphosed progression of the left.

In the second Goetheanum, the two side panels are positioned below the middle panel. Although Rudolf Steiner made a sketch for long windows for the second Goetheanum's auditorium, he did not specify their content. After his death, the decision was made to take up the colors and themes of the windows from the first Goetheanum but place them in the long window spaces sketched for the second Goetheanum.

To each of these twenty-seven window panels, Rudolf Steiner expressed its essence in a couple of words. These words were born as a reply from Rudolf Steiner to Assia Turgeniev. While showing him her sketches of the windows of the first Goetheanum, she had asked him if something should not be written under them. To her we also owe the present windows, which she single-handedly carved in a twenty-year labor of love.

Assia Turgeniev named the windows with the color of a corresponding precious stone. Her example is followed in this book. Color, word, and image conjoin to illumine in modified sunlight the path of initiation. The five colors of the windows may be viewed as a sequence of five stages.

## Subject and Object

To step into the auditorium is to engage in a world drama. The stages of initiation in the human being's relationship to the world are expressed through the colored windows. The *world (Die Welt)* is addressed in each of the captions (with the exception of the Amethyst Window, the theme of which is *time*). It is the world around us that demands the human being's full engagement to discover the individual's true identity. All evolution of consciousness is predicated on separation out from the world, thereby gaining independent consciousness, to then reconnect to the world in reflecting the world back.

The human being's evolving consciousness finds expression in the changing relation between subject and object. The changing balance of subject and object expresses the human being's evolving perception of self and world.

In the path through the windows, a sequence unfolds of five steps of self-knowledge of the polarity of subject and object. The southern windows may be seen to depict the inner path. The northern windows may be seen to depict the outer path. The goal annunciated in the Ruby Window is the integration of the two paths. The Ruby Window's countenance with its earnest and unwavering gaze is carried within the beholder as the other windows are beheld that stand in polar opposition right and left. The north and south windows are polarities to one another of the great polarity of the *subject,* inner thematic aspect of the south windows and the *object,* outer thematic aspect of the north windows, which are to be integrated.

The north and south windows create a symmetry of color but for each color an asymmetry of theme. The light shining through the windows from the north and south is in opposition spatially and qualitatively. The southern light is intense, saturating the sense life—a quality of inner warmth of love. The northern light is diffuse, withdrawn, and rarefied—a quality of an outer sourcing of spirit.

In the first Goetheanum, the symmetry arrangement of the small cupola reversed this juxtaposition of color and theme. The left and right halves of the small cupola were to have been painted with the identical themes but in contrasting "counter" colors. (This intention of Rudolf Steiner's was only partly realized, see chapter 17.) The different colors were to evoke different feelings to the same conceptual theme.

With the windows, the variance of themes to the sameness of color unites the opposite themes in a congruency of feeling-mood. A single mood of color permeates polar opposite themes. The polarity of the thematic imagery in the symmetry of the windows progresses through the steps of the colors of the windows. The progression of the colors of the windows develops a feeling dynamic of metamorphosis out of polarity. A spatial path through the metamorphoses of color and imagery leads the human being through an inner journey as preparation for the drama portrayed on the stage.

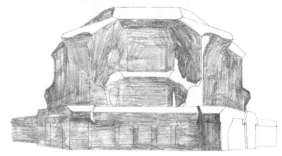

W   *12:30*

## Stage One

Red is the color of initiative, the color with which the rainbow begins. It exults in correspondence to the image of the face's gaze of will into the earnest way of initiation.

*The Ruby Window's* center panel has the caption: *I behold (Ich schaue).*[51] The word caption sequence begins with the act in direct speech of the I perceiving. This window has a few unique features that distinguish it from the rest. 1) It is placed in the symmetry line of the auditorium and outside in the vestibule—joining these two spaces. 2) Its size is greater than the others. 3) The horizontal layout of its triptych is the same as that of the first Goetheanum where all the windows were horizontal. The windows were designed for such a horizontal layout and this placement gives a greater emphasis on the

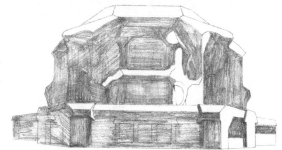

middle panel of the Ruby Window. 4) Its written caption expresses the subject's activity of inner perception in initiation announcing the theme of the path through the windows. This path answers the question of the polar aspect of the object/subject of initiation: the self. 5) Its color is the only color of the windows from the active side of the spectrum.

The Ruby Window's placement compares with a cathedral's west rose window, which commonly, such as at Chartres, has the theme of Christ's second coming as Judge. This theme corresponds to the Ruby Window's. The Guardian of the Threshold appears as judge of the aspirant for initiation.

The larynx chakra's sixteen-petal lotus is emblematically and prominently engraved on the window. The cultivation of the sixteen-petal lotus rests on the development of the objective perception of thought in the human being and nature. Below the larynx chakra motif is the motif of the Archangel Michael subduing the dragon with hands of fiery knowledge witnessed from the heart space of human beings. Above the earnest gaze is depicted the forehead chakra, the place where the godly thought of the human I resides. Imbedded in this cosmic tapestry are the Saturn, Sun, and Moon motifs.

The window depicts the stern requirements of initiation in a three-fold, vertical sequence of the being represented by the face: 1) Above: cosmic being fashions the human being to become a participant spirit; 2) Middle: the unutterable thinking of the cosmos is brought into relationship with the world through the schooling of the eightfold path; 3) Below: witness is born of a cosmic battle for the spirit upon the field of earth.

The left panel has the caption: *It reveals (Es offenbart)*. The right panel has the caption: *It has revealed (Es hat geoffenbart)*. In the left window, the human being encounters the valley of the soul: withered thinking, vain feeling, and hardened will. In the right window, the threshold is crossed: the human being joins in outstretched hands with the sun's rays, and three pairs of angelic beings ascend united in like gesture. The middle window is the way across, the inner path of initiation schooling through the resistance of overcoming oneself. The theme of death and resurrection sounds that would have found its octave in the sculpture intended to be placed opposite the Ruby Window on the stage of the first Goetheanum.

### Stage Two

Crossing the threshold from the Ruby Window vestibule into the auditorium, one meets the complementary color of red: green. With this contrast, the inner threshold is crossed. From the first color in the color spectrum, red, to its complement, green, the jump to the passive, or inner, colors of the spectrum is made. Green is both a color of balance between the two sides of the spectrum and an awakening color as the color of the plant kingdom, the color of the sense world of nature. The red/green contrast itself awakens. In his mystery plays, Rudolf Steiner gave the red and green colors to the sentient soul figure, Philia, who is awake to the sense life.

(In this book, the layout of the north windows on the left pages and the south windows on the right pages is for visual purposes and not sequential ordering. Sitting in the auditorium, left are the north windows and right are the south windows. The task is to relate their polarities—in their progression, west to east, and in their mirroring, north with south.)

*The North Emerald Window* depicts in its central panel the human being standing on a pinnacle of rock in the midst of lightning flashes. Over against these jagged lines of light, a visage emanates over a zigzag descending and contracting path. This panel has the caption: *The world acts to allow the will (Die Welt erwirkt den Willen)*. Rudolf Steiner: "The spirit of weight collects the contradictions that become the resistance in the will of the human being."[52] This characterization that Steiner gave for this window is worked out in the left and right panels: *The will births itself (Es gebiert sich der Wille)* left, and *The will is born (Es ist der Wille geboren)* right. Human will is born out of resistance—ultimately the resistance to matter.

In the left panel, the human being stands as revelation of the matrix of cosmic forces, sun, moon, stars, and of the earth.

In the right panel, the human being becomes creative as an independent being within the cosmic and elemental worlds.

The central panel depicts the human being's awakening, independent will in lightning flashes. The path of descent into the densification of matter becomes the resistance in the will for an ascending path of the renewal of the earth through the Johannine words of the resurrection, "I make all things new."

*The South Emerald Window* depicts in its central panel downward streaming sunlight and upward streaming fire revealing beings imparting and receiving. The human being emerges from a fiery bush, flames of spirit rising from the head. The warmth of fire engenders love for the spirit. The human being's hands rise in receptiveness toward three winged beings. Emissaries of the sun, these beings point with different hand gestures toward the sun's light giving instruction of the spirit.

The center panel has the caption: *The love of the world works* (*Die Liebe der Welt wirkt*). Love in the human being finds the light in the world. Rudolf Steiner: "The light of the spirit becomes the light of man."[53] This description that Steiner gave for this window is worked out in the window's left panel: *And human love arises* (*Und Menschenliebe entsteht*) and in the right panel: *And human love takes hold of him* (*Und Menschenliebe ergreift ihn*). Human love becomes the outer manifestation of wisdom's inner light. Love is the path to the spirit.

In the left panel, the earthly human being directs soul faculties upward for instruction for the earthly life. The spirit self sleeps in the care of higher beings.

In the right panel, the awakened spirit self has become the direct source; the earthly self has become its vehicle, represented as the Mercury column. The human being directs the awakened spiritual faculties downward.

The central panel depicts the act of awakening to the spirit self. The human being is in the bush, or sea, of fire. An own warmth engenders independence, and the fire of love directs to the spirit. The three angelic beings ascend in a threefold instruction of purification awakening to the spirit of the sun. Recognition of the source of one's own fire from the sun and the aspiration of union with the inner light and life of the sun leads to the great Pauline words, "Not I, but Christ in me."

The load of weight and the lift of light are the building's motif. North, the object of the world is produced: will. South, the subject of the world becomes conscious: love's union with wisdom's light. The two great beings, Ahriman and Lucifer, who exist in these extremes must be encountered, integrated, and balanced on crossing the inner threshold. These windows share themes of the pillars Jachin and Boas but for our time.

## Stage Three

With sapphire-blue, the central depth of the passive side of the color spectrum is reached. In contrast to green with its quality of centering, blue has the quality of the periphery. In relation to red, the red/blue contrast is the counter-colors Rudolf Steiner gave to the consciousness soul figure, Luna, in his mystery plays.

*The North Sapphire Window* depicts in its central panel the cosmic drama of the creation of sight with the caption: *The world gives him sight (Die Welt gibt ihm das Sehen)*. The threefold corporeality of astral, etheric and physical is portrayed in the creatures of the Apocalypse of eagle, lion (united in streaming light), and bull (stars).[54] These reflect and incarnate (moons) into the human being (with a crown of triangle, pentagram, and hexagram). The planetary spheres resound in harmony integrating the organization of the human being constituting a place for an own soul nature and I.

The harmonious working of the fourfold human being creates the capacity to perceive and know the world. First, in the left panel, the physical world is seen passively: *And he sees (Und er sieht)*. Then, in the right panel, the spirit world is seen actively: *And he makes himself seeing (Und er macht sich sehend)*.

Sight is the king of the senses that makes the human being a citizen of this world. The healing of the man born blind that occupies the entire Chapter 9 of the Gospel of St. John is done with earth and spittle in a renewal of the original creation of the human being, of Jehovah's creation of Adam related in Genesis. The senses unite the human being with the perceptual will of the manifest world. But to this seeing of the sense world belongs the seeing of the spiritual world without which the result is a state of blindness to the spirit. Christ anoints in the sense world perception of the divine, "Thou hast seen Him," He says to the man born blind. The newly seeing man responds, "I believe"—seeing's source and object seen are one.

Rudolf Steiner wrote the word *thinking (Denken)* over his sketch of the two side panels of the North Sapphire Window and *willing (Wollen)* above his sketch of the two side panels of the South Sapphire Window. The path between the two sapphire window triptychs is the synthesis of thinking and willing in the human organization that has its source in the cosmos.

*The South Sapphire Window* depicts in its central panel twelve human figures, stars, and forms from the world of the zodiac with the caption: *The outer-world in decision (Die Aussenwelt im Entschluss)*. The twelve human figures are the expression of pure will, of the human organism in movement and gesture. The zodiacal forms behind the human figures can be perceived in the human being's astral body.[55] The stars localized in the human figures absorb light (etheric), and the stars with their tails ray out the activity of the light in a dynamic process. The spiritual source and impulse constitute the twelve macrocosmic forms that inform the microcosmic human being's activity.

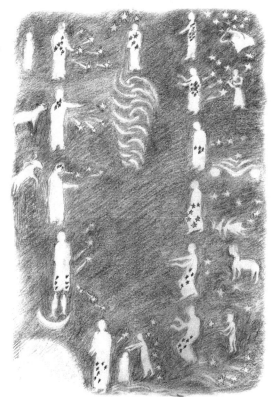

The depiction of the stars is mysteriously mathematical with the numerical properties of the number of stars for each gesture of the zodiac from Aries with three stars to Leo with nine stars. The starry world of intelligence that stands behind the outer-world of appearance manifests in the spoken utterance of deeds depicted in the center panel.

This cosmic event plays out at the human level in the depiction of the left panel: *Deciding (Sich entschliessend)* and right panel: *He has willed (Er hat gewolt)*. The left panel formulates the intent. In the right panel, the intent is carried out. In the right panel, a bullet is depicted in mid-flight (similar to the stars that shoot out from the human forms). From the intention to shoot to the executed act of shooting, the will is engaged. But the hunt is for the bird, intelligence. This intelligence the human being shoots to own and imbue with will. The relationship of the beings in the angelic kingdom is expressed through the bird. This relationship the human being must bring to earth.

In the center panel, the left sequence of five from Cancer to Pisces is the constellations the sun was in at the vernal equinox in the cultural periods of our present epoch from ancient India to the present. The stars for these constellations are in their front space. The right sequence may represent the future beginning with Aquarius. The stars for these constellations are in their backspace. The beings and forces of the constellation of Pisces stand behind our present culture of the earth globe. Our time is a time of decision, a decision of the hunter's game: what will the human being do with this newfound faculty of starry intelligence? The fate of decision is carried in the will, of spiritual thinking's decisive relation to the earth.

## Stage Four

The color opposite red in the spectrum is looked upon, violet. Violet is the last color in the spectrum and therefore a threshold color before the darkness. The threshold of birth and the threshold of death are the themes of the violet windows. Violet is both an inward, calm color and a color of the inner power of sovereignty. A tension is apparent in its placement in the window sequence. Within the spectrum of the sequence, the red/violet contrast is the greatest distance.

*The North Amethyst Window* depicts in its central panel the theme of death and the period of the three-day review of the past life. It has the caption: *It has been (Es ist gewesen)*, which is in present perfect tense describing past action (of being) extending to the present time. The left panel has the caption: *It had become (Es war geworden)*, which is in past perfect tense expressing past action completed before some other past action—the past action of the central panel—the verb *become* meaning "come to be." The right panel has the caption: *It was (Es war)*, which is simple past tense, the essential past with its consequence for the future. The use of the compound tense expresses a movement continuum in past time.

The left panel depicts the moment of death. Rudolf Steiner: "At the moment of death, a light shines forth in the region of the heart and the etheric body, astral body, and I can be seen rising from out of the head. Then for the brief time of about three days the human being sees his whole past as a great tableau of memory pictures."[56]

The right panel anticipates reincarnation. The image of the right panel with the four ravens relates to a specific historical story. It depicts the legend of Frederick Barbarossa (1122–1190), the German Holy Roman Emperor, that tells of his sleep after his death in a cave in a mountain. When the ravens cease to fly around the mountain, he will awaken and return. The principle of reincarnation stands as a polarity over against the event of death. In the past lies the seed for the future.

Death is the will aspect of the future yet expressed in the process of the past tense: the critical moment of death–the memory of the past life–the results of the past life influencing and anticipating a return in the future.

*The South Amethyst Window* depicts in its central panel the theme of birth, the moment of the contract, with the caption: *It arises (Es entsteht)*. The subject *it* is non-referential and no object is present: the verb predominates. The verb *arise* is placed in a time sequence of the verb *to be*: *It will be (Es wird sein)* in the left panel and *It is (Es ist)* in the right panel. The tense progresses: future–coming into being–present. *It* not only places the focus on the verb but lends the activity a context of newness, a quality of beginning.

Rudolf Steiner describes the involved process of incarnation. The human entelechy brings from the spirit realm the pure astral and etheric extract of the fruits of the previous life. In the soul realm, "The germinal human being gathers new astral substance like scattered iron-fillings brought into order by the pull of a magnet." Bell-shaped, this amalgam travels at great speed "searching for parents with the suitable characters and family circumstances." The left panel has this looking, searching quality. The straight-line forms express the outer pressing in of the element of thought.

After conception, "The etheric substance shoots in from north, south, east, and west, from the heights and from the depths, and the etheric body is guided to correspond with the astral form and with the contribution by the parents to the physical body."[57] The right panel has the quality of such waves enveloping the human soul, which is guided into densification of the developing physical organism through pregnancy. The curvilinear forms express the inner pressing out of the element of will.

The Janus-faced being depicted in the central panel reviews the heredity stream and previews the union with the parents of the incarnating soul. With profound and complex interweaving of creative forces, this high being enables the panoramic moment of conception.

Birth is the wisdom of the past yet expressed in a temporal life process of the future that is coming into being, the cause of the coming life with its vision of the future.

The path between the two amethyst window triptychs is the tension of our lives in the calm violet color. Future will is presented in past tense, and the wisdom of the past is presented in future tense. The polar dynamic of time is balanced.

## Stage Five

The heavenly sister of red, magenta, is looked upon. Different names are given this color: peach blossom, incarnate (the color of the newborn baby), purpur or rosa (in German), or magenta. It is hard to reproduce, and the window color in the Goetheanum has an overly orange tone. The magenta color can be seen best in a prism where Goethe originally discovered it or in the bougainvillea flower or tourmaline stone.

Looking through a prism at a speck of light in a darkened room, one sees the rainbow color sequence with green in its middle. Looking through a prism at a speck of darkness against the light (black against white), one sees the colors yellow–red and violet–blue join to produce magenta in the middle.

With magenta, the inner, quintessential realm of the human being is addressed and heralds the spiritual realm embodied by the stage. The green color at the threshold of the auditorium that heralds the world in its sense manifestation is fully completed with its complement of the magenta color. A threshold is crossed from the violet to the magenta-tourmaline windows acknowledged with the architecture of the threshold to the stage, which is initially dark, the curtain closed.

*The North Magenta-Tourmaline Window* depicts in its central panel the human being in a blessing, knowing, awakening, redeeming gesture toward nature with the caption: *The world wafts piety (Die Welt weht Frommsein)*. Nature conveys the experience of piety. A leafed plant (7 + 7 leaves = 14) unfolds a face with closed eyes. Enchanted nature sleeps. Solar rays stream through nature and over the scene. Piety or devotion becomes the religious attribute uniting the human being to redeem the will of manifest nature.

The left and right panels depict a being with the same hand gesture as that of the human being in the middle panel. The Christ with the outpouring of the event of Golgotha encounters first Lucifer and then Ahriman. Piety as redemptive force flows first into the heights and then into the depths. The left panel has the caption, *So he becomes pious (So wird er fromm)*, and the right panel, *Piety works (Die Frommheit wirkt)*.

Three steps in the progression of the consciousness of piety are unfolded: 1) The *world* wafts the *being of piety (Frommsein)*. 2)

The *human being* acquires through the redemption of Lucifer the adjectival attribute *pious (fromm)*. 3) *Piety (Frommheit)* as abstract quality is effective through redeeming Ahriman. What was announced in the central panel as a new act of consciousness toward nature is developed into an objectification of piety in the human being. This state leads over to the human being producing the working of piety in the world. From piety as object to piety as subject, the human being internalizes in consciousness outer nature—a far future consciousness.

*The South Magenta-Tourmaline Window* depicts in its central panel a seated figure: the human being as the thinker, or meditator, with the caption: *The world builds (Die Welt baut)*. The starry realm (two groups of stars: 6 + 8 = 14) of the spirit is met in its intuitive nature as the creative beings of existence. The subject, *world,* is characterized in its activity as the agent, the *builder,* of the human being's form and of the human I.

The left panel depicts a lying figure with the caption: *I behold the building (Ich schaue den Bau)*. Steiner uses the intransitive verb *schauen* but with object (*behold* conveys its objective quality). Imaginative perception internalizes the object world creating that which is inwardly perceived, creating the world further. The right panel depicts a standing figure with the caption: *And the building becomes the human being (Und der Bau wird Mensch)*. Uniting with the world, the I communes with the creator beings of the spiritual world within the temple of the human body.

Three states of consciousness are depicted in the south magenta-tourmaline triptych. The left panel shows the human being lying: object consciousness of the world (ordinary daily consciousness) in which the threshold is concealed. The center panel shows the human being sitting: conscious activity of the world (the path of inner schooling). The right panel shows the human being standing: subject consciousness of world existence (future participatory intuitive consciousness) in which the threshold is revealed.

The path between the two magenta-tourmaline window triptychs is a three-step progression in consciousness from object consciousness to subject consciousness of north, the spirit transparency of the kingdom of nature; and south, the spirit transparency of the temple of the human being.

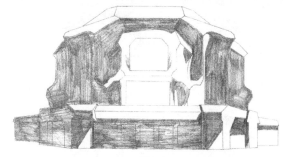

# 14

## Rudolf Steiner's Sculpture: The Representative of Humanity between Lucifer and Ahriman

*The Right Scene:* The Center Figure steps forward. This act initiates the dramatic moment of the right scene (the Center Figure, Lucifer falling, Ahriman bound). The Center Figure separates himself from the matrix of the cliff wall and steps diagonally toward the viewer. This separation from the unified wall and individuation of a freestanding, independent being is the catalyst that separates Lucifer and Ahriman apart.

*Lucifer,* utterly shattered, his levity-generating, balloon-like, externalized organs of ears and larynx, thorax of heart and lung deflated, hurtles in free fall backward, away from the Center Figure, and plunges head down clasping with a powerful, oversized left hand at the cliff wall to break his fall. This grasping action unites him with the earth. His right hand, in counterpoise, touches thumb to forefinger to himself in a gesture of enclosure, control, and wisdom. His differentiated hand gestures mimic the Center Figure but upside down, reversed: his left hand down toward the earth, his right hand up toward his own being. This gesture induces his oversized, voluptuous expansion that wraps around the cliff to connect with the gravity stream—almost sinking the whole sculpture.

*Ahriman,* in total despair, is in crystallized pain from and contracted hatred toward the bright light that penetrates his dark cave like "gold veins" (Steiner) with which he binds

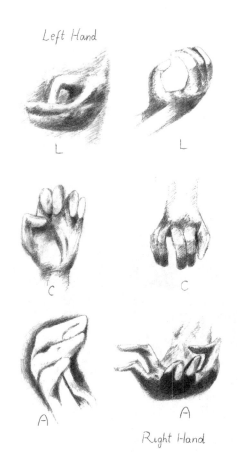

Left Hand

L     L

C     C

A     A

Right Hand

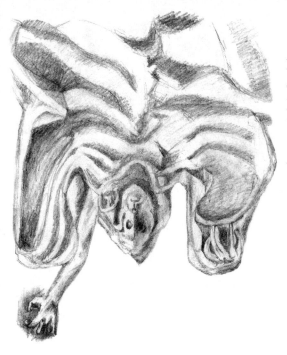

himself. He strains vainly against his bonds reaching up to ward off the light. His right hand contracts from the ground, his left hand contracts from the source of the light. The palm of his right hand pushes back against the earth while the fingers disconnectedly stretch apart and away from the ground in a writhing disconnect from matter. In counterpoise, the raised left hand clenches in a fist the tightly cramped, hard, and empty thinking of materialism. Ahriman is a landscape of tangled twists and turns. His circumscribed space is cramped. His legs with no calves are shortened. One wing sticks into the ground while the other cloaks him, a depiction of materialistic thinking and hidden agenda. Ahriman's gesture of mock imitation of the Center Figure splits open his force of contraction in the lift to the light.

Ahriman's heart is a hollowed space, a denial of the self. In contrast, Lucifer's chest protrudes grotesquely in self-promotion. The Center Figure's heart in rhythmic differentiation unites with his arms and relates to his surroundings.

*The Center Figure* stands apart as a fully three-dimensional figure. All the other figures are reliefs imbedded in the matrix background, whether convex as Lucifer or concave as Ahriman. This environment of reliefs as a quasi two-dimensional world is a spiritual tapestry to the Center Figure's three-dimensional quasi sense-perceptual presence. This contrast presents a revealing drama of the critical relationship between the sense and spiritual worlds. The Center Figure stands free from the spiritual matrix yet, fully cognizant of it, responds. Freedom is possible if spirit is witnessed from the sense world. Lucifer and Ahriman, aware of the Center Figure, respond to divide him into extremes. The Center Figure responds to Lucifer and Ahriman by encompassing their duality in polarity, uniting them in polarity, becoming the Being of polarity. In the sense world lies the possibility to bring duality into relationship uniting them in polarity. The synthesis of duality in polarity is the balanced simultaneity

of opposites—a task possible only in the sense world where freedom to recognize the spirit creates union with the world.

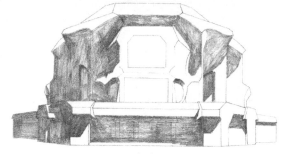

W    *14:30*

*The Left Scene:* To the left of this highly dramatic, radically explosive, dangerously unstable scene of uncontrolled, fast-moving events around a still center of self-control is presented a contained and closed system of binary duality. The static containment of this left scene is further developed in the self-containment of each of the two parts of this scene. Both Lucifer and Ahriman are separately self-contained in their own universe. Each expresses in his form and gesture his essence. Lucifer floats in magnificent self-involvement. His hands are a gesture of magical power. His tentacle-like legs lick into the nether world of Ahriman and wrap around his wrists. With his fishtail-like legs, Ahriman kneels; his bat-like wing folds like an enormous, encrusted seashell along his body; his goat-like horns butt the darkness of his walled, enclosed domain. Bound by Lucifer's legs, Ahriman's hands pull and push, clutch and grab at the restraint. Although fully interlocked, the two beings are equally and fully separate, like a two-piece mechanism or input-output system: duality par excellence. This duality is further emphasized by the frontal portrayal of Lucifer and the profile portrayal of Ahriman. These two planes form a cross holding in a vise the human being in a predetermined course.

The left scene plays out in the matrix of the spiritual landscape lacking in the human being's three-dimensional, sense-perceptible involvement and absent the human being's engagement, awareness, and perception of these beings. If left unrecognized, these being's presence and activities will fully influence and annihilate the human being in a division that leaves no quotient. The left scene as a picture of duality may be seen as an imagination of evil, of the human being without a cardinal center. In contrast, the right scene with its diagonal axis and eternal opportunity for life's creating may be seen as an imagination of the free—it *may*, it is not given—synthesis of polarities, a picture of the good.

Above the fray, witnessing, relating, and objectifying both scenes, is the being of the cliff itself. From this being's head, wings extend and from the wings, hands. It is a willed thought-being that remains in the background as the elemental being of

101

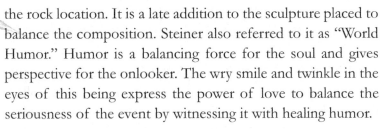

the rock location. It is a late addition to the sculpture placed to balance the composition. Steiner also referred to it as "World Humor." Humor is a balancing force for the soul and gives perspective for the onlooker. The wry smile and twinkle in the eyes of this being express the power of love to balance the seriousness of the event by witnessing it with healing humor.

## The Representative

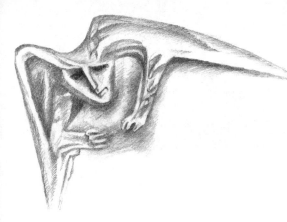

From the peripheral, outer perspective of World Humor, the entire sculpture pivots on the Center Figure and the mastery of eternity in his gaze beyond the confines of space and time, a simultaneous inner-outer perceiving in full knowing. The Center Figure's pronounced and powerful chest with its sensitive, undulating movements initiates and supports the raised left arm and hand that grasps for the idea in Lucifer's realm. This left arm and hand are powerfully muscled to counter gravity and grasp the idea world. Crossing over from the left hand, the right foot strides forward with willed intention into the sense world. Although one movement, the sequence is: first, the heart initiates the impulse; second, the left hand grasps the idea; and third, the right foot strides forward in engagement with the sense world. This dynamic impulse to begin, stretch, and stride is balanced with a containing gesture of the left leg and right arm. The left leg anchors the verticality of the figure to stand. The right hand within the gravity stream grasps the sense world in Ahriman's realm. However, the quality of holding a sense object with the hand is quite different from holding a concept with the mind. The right hand, the hand that leads in the outer activities of life, is powerful in its restraint, placing the sense-world in its rightful place to reveal its open secret.

The human entelechy manifests its free activity in relating opposites. Individuation is realized in the act of integrating the differentiated world. It is the third element that balances opposites. The activity of balancing in syntheses two elements into a third is a new creation. Only in what is free is the new possible. The human being is the only being in the world capable of error and thus freedom. Representing the human being is the creator of the possibility of a new creation.

The image of the Representative of Humanity stands as an apocalyptic revelation that the human being may win identity in the act of knowledge of freedom only in, through, and out of the possibility of error in the extremes of opposition: the duality of evil. The sculpture may be seen to present the metamorphosis of duality into the trinity of the human being.

## *The Sculpture's Genesis in the Preparatory Models*

The greatness of the sculpture may be seen in its special place in Rudolf Steiner's work. Steiner rushed the construction of the first Goetheanum due to the impending world war. The topping-out ceremony for the two domes was held six months after the foundation stone ceremony in an astounding pace of work of the more than 250 workers. Yet the pace of work on the sculpture developed in a careful, step-by-step collaboration with the sculptress Edith Maryon. Ten years after beginning work on the sculpture, he was still working on it in his atelier. Although the sculpture was the culmination of the building, it was held back due to the war. Its designated place in the building remained empty leaving the total space unfinished without its kernel. One can only consider with wonder this caution for the consecration of the sculpture's mystery.

A sequential development of seven models precedes the elm wood sculpture. The models were made with a specially prepared mixture of plasticine and wax that remained pliable. John Wilkes (1930–2011) restored these salvaged models, which allows us to view the sculpture's artistic genesis.

*Drawing: first model*

The first three models were executed in the autumn of 1914. Although Edith Maryon had been at the Goetheanum since the beginning of 1914, Rudolf Steiner did not ask her to begin work on the sculpture until autumn. Thus, at the outset, a reserved aspect of waiting may be observed regarding the sculpture.

1. The first model (14 inches in height) was made by Edith Maryon with indications from Rudolf Steiner. With it, the initiative for the sculpture was set in motion.

2. The second model (16½ inches) was made by Rudolf Steiner. The elements of the first model were developed giving them clarifying structure: a consolidated base with cave; a vertical structure elevating Lucifer's protuberance at its head; the Center Figure placed independently of either form, on a pedestal and the vertical pillar clearly to one side.

*Drawing: second model*

*Drawing: third model*

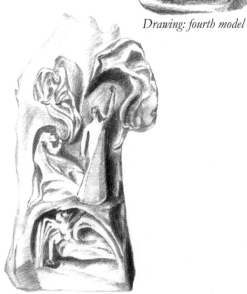

*Drawing: fourth model*

3. The third model (3 feet) was made by Edith Maryon. The previous model's elements were artistically elaborated, unified, and enlarged. The sixth model (6½ feet) was also begun, which was added to as the next two models developed thematically.

4. The fourth model (1½ feet) was made by Rudolf Steiner. There was a pause before its development due to Steiner's schedule. It was made in the opposite time of the year, a half year later in spring, May 1915. As it would turn out, it would become the middle stage of the sequence. It brought a free moment for something thematically new to enter. The cliff was utilized that Maryon had brought forward. The new element of the left scene's dual figures expressed a polar theme to the right main scene: a polarity within a polarity. Rudolf Steiner combined two themes engendering free moral forces in the compositional portrayal (see page 85).

5. The fifth model (1½ feet) made in the following month was a collaboration of Rudolf Steiner with Edith Maryon. What had been primitively sketched with the previous model was worked out in detail. It took on the form of the final version with the exception of the rock being, which was added as the final touch to the final model.

6. The sixth model (6½ feet) was by Edith Maryon showing the cumulative work in increased size and detail.

7. The seventh model (31 feet), a full-size model, was worked on throughout 1916, prepared by Edith Maryon with the help of coworkers and completed by Rudolf Steiner. It was finished in all details and became the copy for the elm wood sculpture.

8. The elm wood sculpture was originally intended to be composed of various kinds of woods reflecting the building (prevented by wartime scarcity). It was begun in the summer of 1917 and was a collaboration of Rudolf Steiner with Edith Maryon along with the help of coworkers. Their efforts continued for four years into 1921. Unfinished, work on the sculpture was halted awaiting further completion of the building. The sculpture was to be completed after its transfer into the Goetheanum. Steiner viewed the building as a total work of art. The restrained quality of the work on the sculpture is again witnessed. A year and a half later the building burned to the ground. Yet the sculpture was saved, and Steiner could pick up chisel and mallet to continue it.

*Drawing: fifth model*

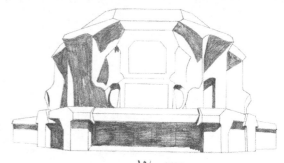

# 15

## *The Malsch Model Building*

The heart of the architectural principle of the second Goetheanum may be revealed if compared with the first Goetheanum and its genesis. A fundamental shift is evident in the architectural principles underlying the two buildings. In the development of the first Goetheanum, the interpenetrating domes provided the key architectural feature of mirroring elements allowing for the rich sculptural forms to develop. These traditional elements of architecture (pillar, capital, and architrave) were brought into movement through the law of metamorphosis and representational forms of the spirit.

The second Goetheanum's mirroring relation of isosceles trapezoid and square directly was brought into movement through metamorphosis in the building's structural elements of load and lift. Pillar, pediment, and frieze described in chapter 4 no longer were the separate elements of the building but the very structure itself.

Together with these elements, the spatial configuration of the first Goetheanum was imbued with the principle of number and ratio. Ratio imbued the space with a dynamic quality that made it live. A look at this central feature will help us ask the question of how ratio in the second building developed as a ratio of load and lift directly. Let us follow Rudolf Steiner's evolving search to form a living space for the spirit.

The genesis of the Goetheanum building impulse that was set alight in the summer of 1907 with Rudolf Steiner's artistic shaping to the space for the society's annual assembly in Munich sparked flames in a number of individuals. A year later in the summer of 1908, Mieta Waller offered financial support for a

In a letter of 28 May 1907
from Marie von Sivers to Edward Schuré:
Dr. Steiner worked on all the arts
and on all the handwork.
He directed everyone: the painters,
sculptors, musicans, carpentors,
wallpaperers, actors, tailors,
stagehands, and electricians.
If he had had the necessary
material and workers available,
he would have brought about
something fabulous in a short time:
the temple of the future.
As it was, he could only sketch ideas,
but they will have a fructifying effect.

temple for the word of anthroposophy. Separately, E. A. Karl Stockmeyer asked Rudolf Steiner for concrete architectural solutions for the seven capital forms portrayed in Munich. Stockmeyer had developed them further as three-dimensional sculptures from Steiner's flatly painted capitals. Stockmeyer executed Steiner's indications in a walk-in dimensional model in his backyard in the small town of Malsch near Karlsruhe, Germany. On the evening of 5 April (the original Easter date) 1909, Rudolf Steiner presided over a ceremony for this small construction.

The structure that Rudolf Steiner sketched for Karl Stockmeyer is an elliptical domed structure. The ellipse equation is a ratio: the sum of the distances from any point on the ellipse to the two foci is a constant—equal to its axis. The ellipse principle can be well demonstrated with two pins, string, and a pencil: tie the string around the two pins; pin them loosely onto a paper and board; pull the loop taut with the pencil's tip forming a triangle, then draw. The heavens move to this ratio. Johannes Kepler discovered that the orbits along which the planets travel around the sun are ellipses with the sun at one focus.

To the principle of the ellipse of the Malsch model building was added a two-space perpendicular interpenetration of an

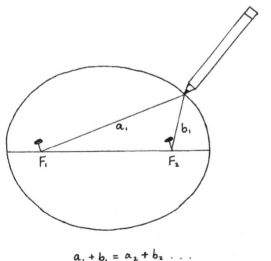

$$a_1 + b_1 = a_2 + b_2 \ldots$$

ambulatory and an inner-space. The ambulatory has red walls upon which are depicted the seven seals from the Apocalypse drawn after sketches by Rudolf Steiner for the Munich Congress.

The ellipsoidal niches of the ambulatory are differentiated, the narrowest distance for the middle seal. The differently spaced pillars are inserted between the seal paintings. From the red wall, the sequence of the seven seals spaced in a tone-like rhythm of pillars impresses itself upon the beholder.

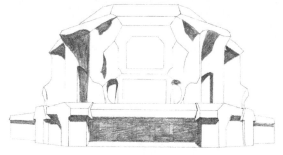

W    16:30

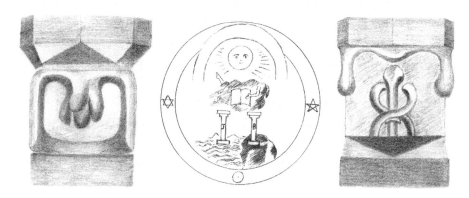

The seven seals portray in pictures the archetypes of Earth's evolution seen by the seer in the soul, or astral, world. The pillar's capitals portray the sculpted form of primal tones heard in the spirit world.[58] A single motif plays through the capitals of a vertical force from below and a carrying force from above that meet and interweave.

The middle of the sequence is shown in the drawing (above) of the relationship of the fourth seal between the Mars and Mercury capitals. The identity of the I through the polarity of the red and blue blood (represented by the two pillars J and B) leads to initiation and the ingestion of knowledge—the practice of which is love. The forces from above and below in the Mars capital invert in the Mercury capital. What descends contains both the force and form that, transformed in the I, ascends.

The seven pillars support the inner-space carrying the blue dome with the golden signs of the zodiac. From Pisces in the west to Aries in the east, the signs of the zodiac in the dome depict the ground plan of ancient temple architecture of the outstretched human being. In initiation science's macrocosm-microcosm correspondences, Pisces represents the feet of the human being and Aries, the head (drawing right).

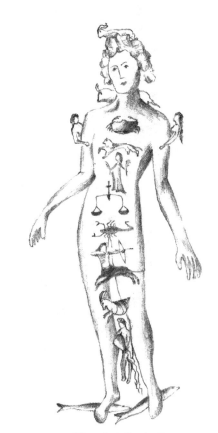

*After a painting by the Limbourg brothers circa 1413*

An elliptical window is set in the southeast side of the dome at a 36° angle for sunlight to enter. The sunlight shines on the north row of pillars, seals, and zodiac. The ocular window is placed directly above the Jupiter pillar on the south side; diagonally opposite is the Sun pillar on the north side. The morning sun of the spring equinox strikes the key of this diagonal polarity from the Jupiter to the Sun pillar. In the course of six hours from nine in the morning to three in the afternoon, the sunlight falls in a shallow arc along the ground in front of the pillars. The great path of the evolution of consciousness of the human being is traversed from the Saturn pillar to the Venus pillar. The sun's projection highlights the sequential progression of the imaginations of the seals from the Apocalypse, the musical inspirations of the pillars' forms, and the intuitions of the zodiacal beings who created the human form from foot to head.

The fourteen pillars stand royally in the space transmitting the weight of the dome to the ground below. The pillars provide a harmoniously differentiated breathing of the space. Rudolf Steiner's indications were for a space hewn in granite with pillars of a green Siberian syenite stone.[59] This ideal was not possible; sandstone, bricks, and plaster were used for the walls and oak wood for the pillars.

In Munich provisionally, the seven pillars were presented once in an 180° arc around the seated assembly and so lacked the symmetry of an axis line. In Malsch, the elliptical ground plan creates a ratio for an axis line. Two sequences of the seven pillars, seven seals, and twelve zodiacal forms in the dome mirror each other left and right creating a symmetry axis with a progression.

Walking around the red, festive ambulatory, one senses the changing ellipsoidal dimensions between the pillars, and the axes of the ellipsoidal arches ray into the center of the space. Standing under the blue dome, one senses the unity of the ellipse ratio's sum. Feeling united with the verticality of the pillars (ideally green) in their symmetrical sequence of forms, one senses integration in a community of initiation knowledge. This structure realized a lasting and living space for the seven pillars of the true Rosicrucian temple.[60] (The Malsch model building is freely rendered on the front cover.)

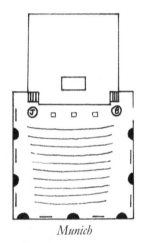

*Munich*

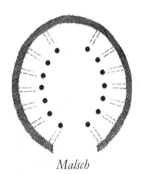

*Malsch*

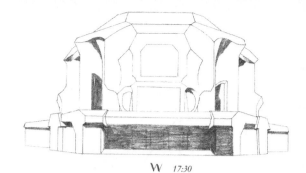

W  *17:30*

# 16

## *Pythagoras's Theorem and the First Goetheanum*

What had begun humbly at Munich and Malsch was brought to grand fulfillment in the first Goetheanum. In the course of seven years, the architectural impulse evolved. For the first Goetheanum, Pythagoras's theorem with the right-angle triangle ratio triple 3, 4, 5 generates the mutual proportions of the building's two cupolas. This ratio deserves a closer look.

*Pythagoras's Theorem* is a relation among the three sides of a right-angle triangle: the square of the hypotenuse (c) is equal to the sum of the squares on the other two sides (a and b). Its celebrated equation is written: $a^2 + b^2 = c^2$. Pythagoras's theorem defines the right angle, and the right angle defines space in the perpendicular joining of vertical and horizontal in the $x$ and $y$ axis of space. The diagonal in two dimensions represents the forward/backward $z$ axis in three dimensions. The right-angle triangle is a dynamic organism interrelating its three lengths. The ratio is made visible through squaring each length. The areas of the squares have a precise relation: the two smaller squares in figure 1 fit perfectly into the larger square in figure 2. This method of geometric rearrangement was the proof Pythagoras used for the theorem. Note in figure 2 the combined shorter lengths of the four right triangles create the large circumscribing square. The relation of the three squares to the single right-angle triangle is shown in figure 3.

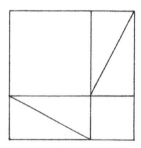

*Figure 1*

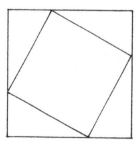

*Figure 2*

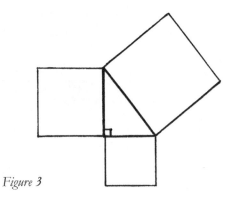

*Figure 3*

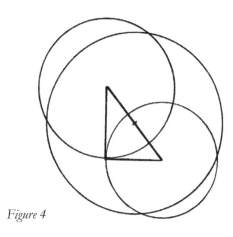

*Figure 4*

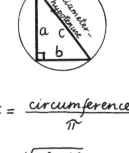

*Figure 5*

$$c = \frac{circumference}{\pi}$$

$$c = \sqrt{a^2 + b^2}$$

This relationship holds true for any figure (circle, pentagon, etc.) constructed with corresponding sides of a right-angle triangle: the sum of the two smaller areas will equal the larger. In the case of the circle, the triangle's sides form the corresponding radiuses; the circles' centers are along the hypotenuse (figure 4). However, squaring the lengths is fundamental for the ratio creating a relation between lengths and areas.

Angulation relates two numbers or directions. The right angle's perpendicularity relates vertical to horizontal. The relation of Pythagoras's theorem to the right angle may be formulated thus: vertical + horizontal = diagonal. That is to say, the diagonal integrates vertical and horizontal.

The right-angle triangle is also related to the circle. Thales's theorem describes a right-angle triangle inscribed in a circle: if the diameter of a circle is the hypotenuse of a triangle that has its opposite angle on the circle's circumference, then that angle is a right angle (figure 5). Thales of Miletus (624–546 BC) lived a short boat trip from Pythagoras of Samos (570–495 BC) and was briefly the younger man's teacher. Their two theorems express the unique ratio of the right-angle triangle. Thales's theorem relates the circle (with its unique properties of the ratio π—circumference to diameter) to the right-angle triangle. In Pythagoras's theorem, the right-angle triangle intrinsically expresses the uniqueness of the right angle.

Rudolf Steiner speaks of Pythagoras's theorem, "Fourfold man is put together as the Pythagorean square."[61] Steiner places the right-angle triangle as an imagination of the interrelated proportions of the human being's four bodies, physical, etheric, astral, and I. To express this interrelation, a metaphoric extended formulation might read: (the horizontal relationship of the physical body and etheric body)$^2$ + (the vertical relationship of the astral body and I organization)$^2$ = (the human being)$^2$ (see page 47). Pythagoras's theorem as an imagination unites the four-fold human being harmoniously.

The higher peripheral I is included as the fifth element in the human being. Rudolf Steiner: "Added to the Pythagorean square is the divine self (spirit self) who descends from above. Thus, a pentagon has been added to the square."[62] This fifth element is the bearer in the human being of the possibility of free will and therefore of decision, error, crises, and evil.[63]

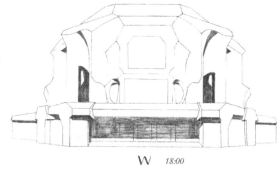

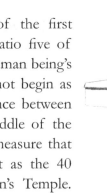

*The Genesis of the Building Plan* of the first Goetheanum begins with this distance of the ratio five of the Pythagorean triple 3, 4, 5 expressive of the human being's fifth principle, the spirit self.[64] However, it did not begin as a ratio but as a measure of distance. The distance between the middle of the large cupola, $M_L$, and the middle of the small cupola, $M_S$, was the only given, the only measure that Rudolf Steiner gave for the building. He set it as the 40 holy cubits of the middle section of Solomon's Temple. Metric measurements were used: 21 meters (69 feet) with 1 cubit = 52.5 centimeters (20.62 inches)—the royal cubit.

West $M_L$ ───── 40 holy cubits / 21 meters ───── $M_S$ East

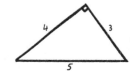

*Figure 1*

The ratio of the stage circle to auditorium circle was proposed as 3 : 4. Carl Schmid-Curtius, the architect in charge of the building, arrived at this proportion as a quite natural solution based on studies for the requirements of a stage-auditorium (with seating capacity for nine hundred). Rudolf Steiner affirmed his proposal.

The ratio 3 : 4 for the radius of the two circles with middle points $M_L$ and $M_S$ creates the measure $M_L M_S$ (the 40 holy cubits) as ratio 5 for the 3, 4, 5 lengths of a right triangle triple (figure 1). With $M_L M_S$ as 21 meters (69 feet) these ratios then measured: radius of the large cupola, $R_L$: 17 meters (55.8 feet—32.4 cubits); radius of the small cupola, $R_S$: 12.4 meters (40.7 feet—23.6 cubits).

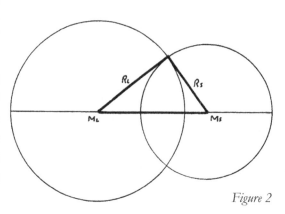

*Figure 2*

Choosing the ratio 3 : 4 determined that $R_L$ and $R_S$ met at a right angle (figure 2). Therefore, their meeting point intersects the circumference of the circle with diameter $M_L M_S$ (figure 3). The simplicity of the triple 3, 4, 5 interrelates the three ensuing circles: the two cupola circles and the middle circle around the original measure engendering a space filled with dynamic life.

The single measurement for the building of the distance between the domes set the key for the two domes' interlocking polar relationship. It is the human being's fifth principle of the spirit self that relates the polar elements of the physical to the spirit. Pythagoras's theorem gave the ratio for this relationship.

*Figure 3*

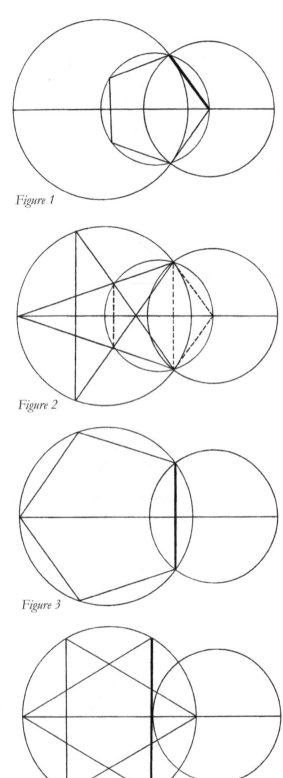

Figure 1

Figure 2

Figure 3

Figure 4

*Pentagon and Hexagram* find their properties thus quite naturally inscribed in the building.

Figure 1: The radius of the small circle (cupola) forms the measure for the pentagon inscribed in the middle circle. The pentagon is the forming principle of the middle circle, yet it takes its measure from the small circle.

Figure 2: From the middle circle's inscribed pentagon, a pentagram can be constructed in the large circle. This pentagram relates the large circle to the middle circle.

Figure 3: The large circle also relates itself to the small circle through the properties of five. The line joining the points of intersection of the two cupolas is the measure for a pentagon inscribed in the large circle.

Figure 4: The tangent to the small circle forms the basis for a hexagram in the large circle. This hexagram relates the large circle to the small circle.

*The Number Principle* of three, six, and twelve infuses and forms the small cupola: three is the ratio of its radius; six is the division of its diameter; twelve is the number of its pillars.

Five is the ratio of the interpolating middle circle. Around its measure with ratio five, the rest of the building was built.

The large cupola relates to the rest of the building with these numbers five and six, but its forming principle is the ratio four for its radius and the number seven for its pillars (or fourteen for the two times seven symmetrical pillars)—the evolving aspect of evolution (seven) on the earth (four).

The path through the symmetry axis of the first Goetheanum leads from the large cupola with its ratio four, the created world, and its seven pillar forms, to the small cupola with its ratio three, the perfection of the Trinity, and its six pillar forms. The path from the past to the future leads through the present, the place of intersection of the two cupolas. From the center of the auditorium circle to the center of the stage circle is the path for the human will to unite and integrate the two worlds of the cupolas. This place of the present held the ratio five and the pentagram expressive of the human being's essence and cardinal quality of free will. Affirming and echoing the geometry of the number five were the twenty-six columns—all five sided (see appendix I).

112

W  *18:30*

The geometry of the human being was inscribed into space with the first Goetheanum. Rudolf Steiner: "Between the astral body and the etheric body lies number. The astral body counts, counts by division, counting the etheric body. The astral body forms the etheric body through number."[65] The measure of the first Goetheanum truly measured the archetypal human being.

In an autumnal mood, the sun having just set behind gathering storm clouds on the evening of the 20 September 1913, the ceremony was held for the laying of the foundation stone. With elemental drama, lightning and thunder neared and rain began to fall as the foundation stone followed the sun into the earth. The document to be sealed in the copper double dodecahedron foundation stone was read and a rite enacted tapping with a hammer the count of four numbers. The great beings of the numbers of the building and of the human being were called out in the count of 3, 5, 7, and 12.[66]

*The Mystery of Metamorphosis* from the first building's internal aspect to the second building's external aspect is great.

Rudolf Steiner's search for a form with an interrelating polar dynamic progressed from the ellipse ratio for Malsch to two interlocking domes for the first Goetheanum. The relationship of the domes evolved, arrived at through cooperation with others. The plan submitted for the Johannes Bau was for two spheres inscribing and circumscribing dodecahedrons. The engineer Alexander Strakosch proposed this solution.

The polar dynamic of great movement and great rest of the second Goetheanum's two interlocking parts and the experience of angle and distance in the approach to the building have an ordering and enlivening effect, a living equation of sequential synthesis—like speech in eurythmy.

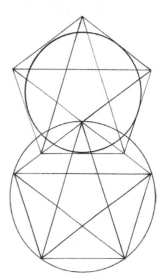

*Alexander Strakosch's ground plan for the Johannes Bau*

Rudolf Steiner created nine inches (median) tall eurythmy figures cut out of wood and painted. Lines and planes of forces, relations of directions, concentration of pressures, and the ratios of its three aspects of dress, veil, and muscle tension of each sound figure combine to express a cosmic dimension of form and movement—for eurythmy to incarnate the audible into the perceptible. The features of these figures have similar characteristics to the forms of the second Goetheanum. Eurythmy as seed in the first building blossomed in the second.

*After a sketch by Rudolf Steiner: stage curtain scenery with E-Ah-O motif*

*After a sketch by Rudolf Steiner: stage curtain scenery with Rosicrucian motif*

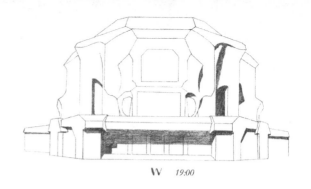

# 17

## A Polar Color Space

*Red and Blue* played a significant role in the beginnings of Rudolf Steiner's architectural impulse. For the interior decoration of the Congress hall in Munich, not only were the walls red, but the ceiling also was draped with red cloth. It gave the space a heightened quality of festivity.

The anthroposophical art rooms in Munich and Berlin were forum spaces for exhibitions, performances, and festivals. They were draped with muted red sackcloth for the walls and ceiling and even the chairs were painted red. These rooms were warm and comfortable social spaces for events.

For the branch room in Berlin, four values of blue were used. The door, floor, chairs, and speaker's table (on which was a bouquet of red roses) were painted a dark blue. The walls were a little lighter rich blue. The window curtains were a light blue. The ceiling was draped with pale blue cloth that hung in waves and was tied in bunches at the ceiling's edge. It gave the space the inner quality of study and contemplation.[67]

Red and blue became united in Rudolf Steiner's further architectural development. In Malsch the walls were red, lifting the perceiver upright, and the cupola a weightless blue. In Steiner's drawing for the Johannesbau in Munich, the walls of the large cupola were red, and the walls of the small cupola were blue. In the first Goetheanum, this color combination was placed in the small cupola. The Madonna colors of red (life) and blue (consciousness) came together in perfect balance: the consciousness of life that becomes the life of consciousness.

115

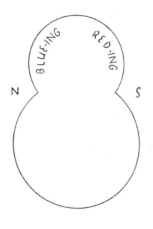

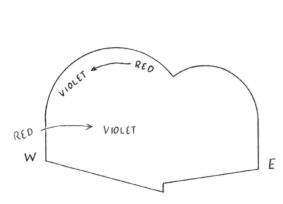

*A Symmetry Color Axis* was created in the first Goetheanum through the meeting of blue and red in the small cupola. The small cupola was to have a right (south), left (north) symmetry with the forms of the motifs mirrored in "counter-colors." Complementary colors are not meant with this term as there was no green in the small cupola. In the small cupola, the colors were to be taken from the night spectrum joining red to blue/violet. "Peach blossom in the middle and around it grouped the counter-colors red-yellow on one side and blue-violet on the other. You can already see how I have made a beginning by painting the red angel on Christ's right side, which is the counter-color of the blue angel on His left. You can also study the different attitude I have given the red angel. This was simply demanded by the red. So I want you to adapt the attitude of the figures you paint on the other side in counter-colors to the character of these colors" (R. Steiner to J.M. Bruinier).[68] The red, yellow, and blue on the right side were to be mirrored on the left side: darker blue, lighter blue, and orange with the exact nuances of the counter-colors weaving between the reds and blues. Since the red/yellows dominate on the right side (south) of the small cupola, the blue/violets would dominate on the left side (north). On the stage, spirit was to be dramatized.

*A Horizontal Color Axis* may be seen created in the large cupola. The colors were to be taken from the day spectrum where the law of complementary color exists. The colors of the large cupola progressed through the rainbow sequence from violet in the west to red in the east. This direction is a polarity to the color sequence of the windows, which progressed from the red window in the west, to the green, blue, and violet windows toward the east. The color sequence of the large cupola and the reverse color sequence of the windows created a horizontal midline axis. In the auditorium, the audience would have felt the cathartic experience of the mystery plays.

*A Frontal Color Axis* joined the two cupolas at the curtain. Before the beginning of a play, the curtain would have been hung with a large painted scene that Rudolf Steiner had sketched. For the mystery plays, the scenery displayed the Rosicrucian journey. For eurythmy performances, the scenery displayed the theme of E-Ah-O. In the frontal plane, the colors engaged the human being in the topical theme to be addressed on the stage.

These curtain sceneries (drawings, page 114) depict the threshold. The E-Ah-O scenery shows a sequence of three portals opening the eurythmic space. The left portal darkly asserts itself, and a column of smoke rises above it indicating the activity within. In contrast, the right portal is an enclosed space for two pairs of angelic beings; one pair face each other with hands and wings behind them in the rounded arch; the other pair join arms in front within the doorway. The middle portal is the hinge in this sequence of metamorphoses; its doorway is darkened, but its arch is radiantly open; in the open arch, a pair of angelic beings raise their arms in the eurythmy sound gesture "ah" of invitation. The colors in Rudolf Steiner's original must be seen to appreciate the drawing's exquisite and dramatic quality of engagement.

W    *19:30*

The curtain scenery for the mystery plays depicts the seeker after knowledge standing before a threshold of water between two hills. Behind the pilgrim, the path that was followed winds around one hill. In front, a second ascent towers above. A first Goetheanum-like building crowns its summit from which emanates the Rosicrucian motif. The ferryman waits to enable the crossing of the threshold.

With the event of a performance, the house lights would dim, the curtain would open, and a new relationship to color would flood the stage. For eurythmy, Rudolf Steiner gave detailed directions for the lighting. A differentiation of color lighting would come from below (footlights) and from above (behind the pillars) creating a diffuse, atmospheric color space. In this color space, the eurythmist in colored costume would give expression in movement to poetry and music.

## Color in the Second Goetheanum

How color would have entered the second Goetheanum remains a question as Rudolf Steiner died before he was able to model the building's interior. The attempts over the years to solve this need grace the building (see appendix II).

Whether concrete's grey color would have remained the final choice for the building's exterior color is also a question.

117

The color treatment of the façade and the roof surfaces was to be adapted to the landscape as outlined in the Solothurn county administration's conditions for the building permit. The Norwegian slate for the roof was carried over from the first building. After removing the molding, the concrete minimally would have been treated. The question is of interest as the exterior of the second Goetheanum played a far greater role than it did in the first Goetheanum, which even so had distinguishing wood coloration due to the choice of wood and the predominance of the slate-covered domes.

Color inside a building relates the human soul to the spaces in the building. Color on the outside of a building relates the building to its surroundings. A color added to the building would then be an earth tone with reference to its location. Another approach is to retain the natural coloration of the building material.

In the case of the Goetheanum, the color of concrete matches the grayish coloration of the Jura limestone cliffs behind the building. Concrete, after all, is made out of limestone.

The choice of concrete for the building was a major, and for the time, radically innovative decision for Rudolf Steiner, fundamentally influencing the building's design. The material once chosen was a determining factor in forming the quality of the building. The convex requirement of the additive nature in forming this moldable material gave rise to mold forms with plane surfaces with edges and angles. In contrast, the concave demands of carving wood in the first building required the excess be pared away. The outer appearance and coloration of concrete in the second building is telling of the building's greatness in the use of this material at the dawn of modern architecture, which became enthralled with this chameleon material.

The art of making concrete has been discovered and lost through succeeding periods of history. In 1974 the French materials scientist and inventor Joseph Davidovits put forward an expert and plausible argument for the great pyramids to have been built with poured, or cast stone, concrete.[69] Perhaps the resurgent use of concrete parallels an older use of the material but in a new art form.

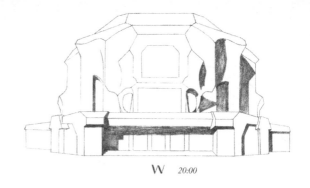

# 18

# *The Foundation Stone*
# *in the Earth and in the Heart*

In the space of ten years and three months, the first building and then the second building received their inaugurations. The foundation stone, or corner stone, for the first building was laid in the open earth with the few representatives and initial coworkers for the building project present. The foundation stone for the second building was placed in the hearts of over eight hundred people who came to witness the event. The walls of the carpenter's hall, where the ceremony was held, were partly removed to hold the overflowing assemblage. The two inaugurations were the foundation stones for a space created for the spirit. Their metamorphic polar presence may be seen to act as the sustaining support for the work entered into in the name of anthroposophy.

## *The Foundation Stone in the Earth*

The progression of forms in the first Goetheanum was from west to east, from the large dome to the small dome. Rudolf Steiner spoke of the difference of construction of the two circles of the domes. The large dome was the simple circle construction of points of equal distance to the center. It was a unity and consolidated the experience of self. The circle is an exact imagination of self-consciousness of the ordinary centered self—at least if so constructed.

The smaller circle was constructed quite differently: a pair of points, one in and one outside the circle, related to one

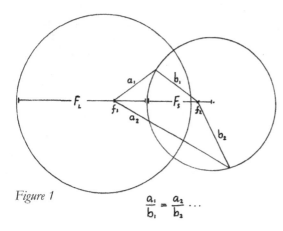

Figure 1

$$\frac{a_1}{b_1} = \frac{a_2}{b_2} \ldots$$

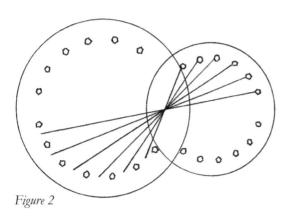

Figure 2

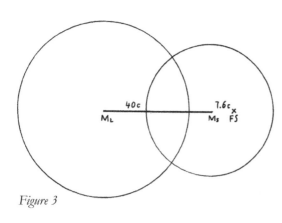

Figure 3

another through division. It is called a *division circle*. The division quotient must be the constant of the two lengths between the two points and the circle. Figure 1 shows the division circle construction with points $f_1$ and $f_2$ arbitrarily chosen. The distances $a_1$ divided by $b_1$ must equal the distance $a_2$ divided by $b_2$. $F_L$ and $F_S$ are the possible locations for the foci points for the construction of a division circle.

Thus, a circle was created from a reference outside it. The division circle is an exact imagination of the higher self, which transcends the limits of the lower self paying heed to the world to which it is connected. (Rudolf Steiner spoke in general terms, not referring to specific points for the construction of the small circle.)

The two cupolas are an imagination of the path of the lower to the higher self. Rudolf Steiner: "Because the forms express a movement from west to east, they directly express the path of the lower to the higher self."[70] On the stage, the spirit striving of the human being was to be dramatized.

Similarly, the building's sculptural elements proceed from west to east. Rudolf Steiner: "Imagine uniting eurythmically what is expressed in the large cupola and then dancing into the small cupola and from there raying out what is danced: then the twelve pillars and cupola would arise of itself."[71]

As much as the large cupola meets the small cupola, so also the small cupola meets the large cupola. Through the symmetry line of the building there is a crossover or reversal from the large cupola to the small cupola. The pillars in the two cupolas interrelate progressively toward one another. In the large cupola, the pillars progress from west to east. In the small cupola the pillars progress from east to west. Both cupolas meet at the rostrum. Through the speaker's rostrum, the columns of the small cupola align with the spaces between the columns of the large cupola on the opposite side of the axis line.[72] The small cupola is the mirror inversion of the large cupola, its six pillars the inner aspect of the seven pillars (figure 2).

The foundation stone for the building was placed in the ground on which the symmetry axis of the building was then drawn. Its location is 7.62 cubits (13 feet) east of the middle of the small cupola *(FS* in figure 3).

120

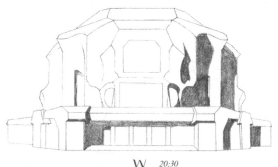

The position of the foundation stone is mysterious for it must generate the rest of the building. It is the source for the building idea from which the rest of the building takes its cue. However, the movement of the building is to the foundation stone; the movement is toward the source, not from it. The source of our earthly person is our heavenly part toward which we orientate our steps.

The division circle's two construction points must fall such that the one point may be anywhere in the larger circle ($F_L$ in figure 1), but the second point within the small circle may only be placed up to the middle point of the small circle ($F_s$). Were a point chosen on the further half of the small circle away from the large circle, the division would not remain a constant. Thus, although within the small circle, the location of the foundation stone lies outside the construction coordinates of the small circle. The foundation stone presents a third orientation point to the two circles. What then does it orientate to?

The focus of the building is the sculpture, the consecration of knowledge of the polarity of evil, which would have stood partly between the end columns of the small cupola and partly in its own alcove and vault. This vault presented a third entire organism of architrave forms. Above and in front of this vault was the third metamorphosed building motif. The second metamorphosed building motif was in the proscenium arch above the rostrum. The first building motif was announced outside the building above the entrance to the middle level. The three building motif forms (drawing, page 74) herald each of the three spaces: auditorium, stage, and sculpture.

The position of the sculpture may be seen to hold a relation to the position of the foundation stone. The foundation stone position is midway between the center of the small circle and the sculpture. Although it may variously be considered where exactly the sculpture would have been placed, the leeway is minimal. With near perfect exactitude it may be imagined at the position of the Center Figure's heart from where the movement source for the entire sculpture originates—kernel for the entire building. The foundation stone in this imagination relates the sculpture to the small circle. That is, the foundation stone relates the impulse of the sculpture to the higher self of each human being.

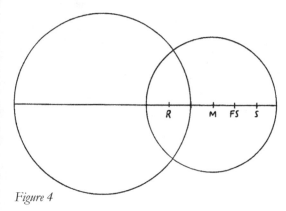

*Figure 4*

Figure 4 shows the critical placements of *S:* sculpture, *FS:* foundation stone, *M:* middle of small cupola, *R:* rostrum, and the intersection of the large circle's circumference with the small circle's diameter. Together these five positions divide the diameter of the small cupola into six equal parts. (A slight margin of error is present, six inches. For exact measures, see Carl Kemper, *Der Bau.*)

## The Foundation Stone in the Heart

The foundation stone for the Anthroposophical Society was laid in the hearts of its members Christmas Day 1923. The ground upon which the new building would rise already held the foundation stone for the first Goetheanum. The founding of the Society was at the same time the renewal of the building impulse. The Society and building were founded together as parts of a greater whole and remain inexorably united. (This connection of building and society is also apparent in the first Anthroposophical Society and the first Goetheanum. They arose together in 1912–13 and ceased together in 1922–23.)

Rudolf Steiner presented the lift and load motif for the second Goetheanum New Year's Day 1924 at the end of the Christmas Conference—an eight-day octave—after first presenting the Foundation Stone mantric verse. As we shall see, the entire conference was required to place the foundation stone. Only then could the building itself be addressed. The Goetheanum and the Anthroposophical Society are an undivided whole: the content poured into the vessel, the vessel built around the content. Steiner cautioned that the Society could not stand without the Goetheanum.

The foundation stone of the first Goetheanum was composed of two dissimilar-sized copper dodecahedrons joined together. It was placed in the ground opposite, or polar, to the directions of the small and large cupolas. The smaller copper dodecahedron aligned west in the ground in the direction of the large cupola, and the larger dodecahedron aligned east in the ground in the direction of the small cupola.

Such an inverse relation to the second building may also be found in the Foundation Stone mantram. This mantric verse is divided up into four units, or panels. Each panel has two parts, or stanzas. The first stanza names the addressee,

122

"Human Soul," and then continues for twelve lines. The second stanza has seven lines before addressing at the end the spirits of nature (of its elements and rhythms: seasonal, lunar, and diurnal). The first stanzas of the panels speak to the human soul and the second stanzas speak of the world of the Trinity. This relation is inverse to the building's ground plan of the progression through the building from the auditorium (world) to the stage (human being), from outer world evolution to inner consciousness. Rudolf Steiner called the Foundation Stone mantram the universal dodecahedron joined with the human dodecahedron.[73]

The version of the Foundation Stone mantram that Rudolf Steiner used during the conference was differently composed compared to the version he submitted for publication. The version he used had the first parts of the three panels grouped together, the trio of stanzas for the human soul. The second parts of the three panels, the trio of stanzas for the Trinity, were also grouped together. The fourth panel was placed between these two groupings uniting their polarity of human being and world. This final panel relates the microcosm to the macrocosm in the Christ. The polarity dynamic was placed foremost in this compositional presentation of the mantric verse.

Rudolf Steiner spoke this compositional organization on the morning of Christmas Day as dedication. In the succeeding seven mornings, different extracts were given from the mantram. A part of the mantric verse was given from which two separate selections of lines were taken from the verse and placed together. Two separate facets from the verse were extracted and fused. A mantric path within the Foundation Stone developed uniting its polarity. A sevenfold sequential progression of verses unfolded, "The Rhythms of the Foundation Stone."[74] In the Foundation Stone's primary polarity arranged in a threefold structure was a secondary polarity arranged in a dynamic sevenfold sequence.

On the evening of New Year's Day, the Foundation Stone was given a ninth time, the second time in its entirety. In this last presentation of the mantram, for the first time the compositional form of the published version was given, which emphasized and placed foremost the mantram's threefold form.

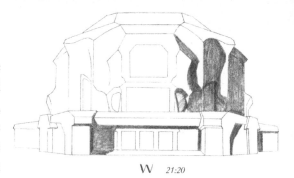

W    21:20

THE INCARNATION
13 LINES
CHRIST IN US
12 LINES

MICRO
DODECAHEDRON
– TRIUNE SOUL
12 LINES

MACRO
DODECAHEDRON
– THE TRINITY
7 LINES

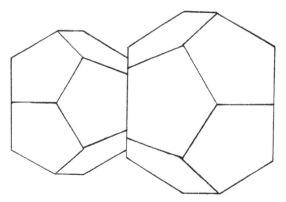

The Goetheanum came into being with the Foundation Stone mantric verse, each informing the other. The term for the title of the mantric verse was a building term: *foundation stone*. The building motif was presented only after the seven-day celebration for the laying of the Foundation Stone. The second building was to have all Rudolf Steiner's consideration and experience of architectural design gained in the years of the creation of the first building. The second building was raised by a third, which gave the front with the three-partitioned vestibule of the west façade a fully presented part of the building. The building received a clear threefold distribution in its three levels.

The Foundation Stone mantram's threefold structure may be imagined corresponding to the three levels of the building. The microcosm of the human being's threefold bodily organization of limbs, heart/lungs, and head addressed in the Foundation Stone corresponds to the three levels of the vestibule. A possible correspondence with the Foundation Stone is the correlation of the three vestibule levels with the addressee of the three stanzas: "Human Soul." It is the ancient word "Know Thyself" renewed in a threefold form.

It may be imagined that the building addresses the human soul in the Foundation Stone mantram as the human being enters and penetrates the building level by level revealing the nature of both. The vertical and horizontal distribution of spaces in the Goetheanum may be imagined as the polar spatial form of the threefold balance of the human soul within the temple of the human body permeated by and united with the world of the Trinity found in the Foundation Stone meditation.

Rudolf Steiner: "The Foundation Stone received its substance from universal love and human love; its picture image, or form, from universal imagination and human imagination; its radiance from universal thoughts and human thoughts." In each case, the universal works in the individual and the free individual in the universal human being. The soil into which this magical structure was lowered were the human hearts beating in "harmonious collaboration" for the will of anthroposophy directed toward "the light of thinking that can ever shine toward us from the dodecahedral Stone of love."[75]

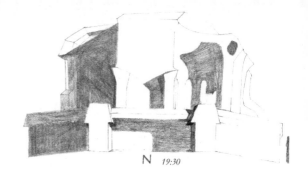

# *19*

## *The Exoteric Purpose of the Building*

### *Coming of Age*

At Christmas 1923 in the Statutes, also called Principles, of the Anthroposophical Society, Rudolf Steiner gave an appellation for the new building: *Free High-School for Spiritual-Science—Goetheanum (Freien Hochschule für Geisteswissenschaft—Goetheanum)*. With this title, the building-to-be received its calling: *an independent school for the spirit.*

The name and idea of a school for spiritual science had been part of the first building's history and a long-standing goal of Rudolf Steiner's. However, its realization had met with scant success. As part of the refounding of the society and the renewal of the building, Steiner placed the school idea center-stage. The single condition for membership in the Anthroposophical Society was formulated with the express purpose to foster the school: "To recognize the validity of an institution such as the Goetheanum as a School of Spiritual Science."[76] The Goetheanum was to be such a school, its name the heading for the school. Building and Society would have the school as their mission. The Anthroposophical Society would be the entrance to the three classes that Steiner planned to create. Society and classes would be divided into research sections of culture, similar to the colleges of a university.

With this designation, Rudolf Steiner placed the new building-to-be within the historical stream of the cultural imperative of learning institutions.

On the one hand, the school idea has its origins in the mysteries, that wellspring of the god's revealed wisdom through clairvoyant consciousness taught in the mystery centers of antiquity. In Eleusis, the Eleusinian mysteries were taught through enactments of the human soul's relation to nature in the rite of Demeter and Persephone. In Ephesus, the mysteries were taught of the formation of speech in the micrologos human being out of the macrologos through the rite of the moon goddess Artemis. The Epic of Gilgamesh tells of the Sumer king's search for the land of the dead in a center of wisdom far to the west in what is today central Europe. The fabled teaching of planetary evolution of the seven holy Rishis in ancient India defined that ancient culture.

On the other hand, the school idea has its origins in the humanly acquired knowledge of the intellect. Spiritual revelation of clairvoyant faculty united with the intellectual faculty creates the clair-thinking, or spiritual thinking, of spiritual science. The idea of an anthroposophical school unites these polar strands of culture. A renewal of the mysteries is sought in a culture of initiation through the development of new faculties of knowledge, of the life of ideas leading to an imaginative consciousness.

The virginal, self-creating flame of thinking as the victorious instrument of culture coalesced around the figures Socrates, Plato, and Aristotle. Their centers of learning, the Agora (market place), Academy, Lyceum (epithet for the sun god Apollo), and the Museion University of Alexandria spread a creative light through the souls of human beings for millennia to come. This creative ferment of the intellectual, spiritual flame found further development in Cluny, Chartres, Paris, and in the court school of Charlemagne in Aachen. In the development of Scholasticism and the Seven Liberal Arts, thinking became imbued with the life of Christianity. The creative thinking in these historical junctures of culture created new impulses in classical and medieval architecture.

The architectural impulse behind the Goetheanum may be viewed as such a further development in architecture. The architecture of the Goetheanum springs from anthroposophical thought. Anthroposophy as a spiritual palladium provides a sure key to unlock the faculty of thinking's

126

source for a new culture of initiation. The radical adventure of the human being's engagement with the world can find its orientation inspired through the spirit of anthroposophy. The Goetheanum's role then would be similar to that of Ephesus, the Lyceum, or Cluny but for our times.

But the original intention for the School with its three classes abruptly ended. Rudolf Steiner's early death cut short the possibility of its development. A conference center replaced the school ideal for the building, and the requirement for admission to the Anthroposophical Society became, "To acknowledge the value of Rudolf Steiner's work in the world."[77] Without the School, the organs of Anthroposophia, building and social bodies, went their separate ways.

## "School" Today

Schooling with an esoteric dimension seeks not only to learn about the world but discovers in the world the human being in overcoming the subject-object dualism. It seeks to grow-together with the world creating the transformational goal of education. The human being becomes the measure of the world, and the world becomes the source of that measure. The way of learning is through the world in experimentation and research through the methodology of spiritual science. The living fermentation of a school creates the atmosphere conducive for research. The First Class of the School places a bridge from self to world through the practise of knowledge.

In the autumn of 1920, Rudolf Steiner spoke at the Goetheanum of the building's connection with the Waldorf School founded in Stuttgart in the prior autumn of 1919. He spoke of the goal of a "World Association of Schools," the founding of schools throughout the world in the pedagogical spirit of the Waldorf School. "We have to be able to extend this school (the Waldorf School) until we are able to move into higher education of the kind we are hoping for here (at the Goetheanum) [...] supporting that which is necessary in order to work here on the further extension of all the separate sciences in the spirit of spiritual science."[78]

Rudolf Steiner inaugurated the First Class of the School of Spiritual Science in the early part of 1924 between the Christmas Conference and the creation of the model for the new building. In the first few pages of the *First Class Lessons*, Rudolf Steiner refers to the School's inauguration with the word *school* twenty-one times, each time developing the idea in a sequence from restoring the School, through recognizing one's own shortcomings of self-will, to finally identifying oneself with the spirit of the School.

Rudolf Steiner sought to establish "a modern mystery school" where "the real purpose of the Goetheanum is that every individual shall be able to find there whatever it is his own soul is striving for in a general way."[79] The Sections were to provide guidance and deepening in the specific arts and sciences. But such a modern mystery school requires an initiate teacher.

Today, with the advance of materialism's authoritarian and instrumental thinking eradicating the practice of freedom—creating out of nothing—in the computer-centered automation of education, our cultural identity is deteriorating before our eyes. It is becoming evident that the learning institutions of the future will not provide the bases upon which the human-centered ideal that began in the Renaissance to develop an objective self-consciousness of matter and spirit will have a place at all. Without this cultural creative capacity at the heart of learning, there will be little to draw upon in the way of future capacity for the furtherance of individual initiatives.

Yet in the death of materialism must the new life of the spirit be sought for new life is found in the depth of death. A university addressing the life of the thinking spirit would renew culture. Spirit is culture and without it there can be none. The disciplines of a university down to their last detail would reveal new wellsprings of meaning through the science of the spirit—for we live in a world of the meaning of things. A university as the meeting place for the spiritual life would cultivate new capacities and foster new life for individual initiatives.

The latent genius and spiritual truthfulness of the architecture of the Goetheanum has the potential to fashion that for which it was built.

Rudolf Steiner spoke about his plans for the building on the mornings of 31 December 1923 and 1 January 1924 bookmarking the anniversary of the burning of the first Goetheanum New Year's Eve 1922–23. On 31 December

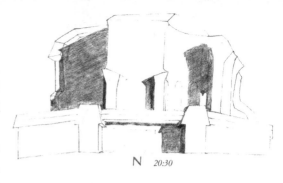

N   20:30

1923, he spoke about the internal distribution of spaces; on 1 January 1924, he spoke of the outside façade. The activity of the inside gave shape to the form of the outside, the second building encompassing the memory of the first building.

An expansive openness still pervades the Goetheanum grounds, a universal quality of a university-school campus. The building is built for a community in all branches of the arts and sciences. Building and grounds provide a location for the community, and the community would give meaning to the building and grounds. A school-university would provide such a consciously formed, critical mass of individuals on site lending life to the cosmopolitan spirit of the Goetheanum.

Out of the fire that consumed the first Goetheanum with its rich interior, the metamorphosed second Goetheanum with its malleable exterior orientates outward to the world. The spirit flame of the second Goetheanum's forms evokes a new language of the human being's relationship to the world. Rudolf Steiner describes how spiritual light streamed up from the burning first Goetheanum, its living content inscribed into the etheric realm. Imaginative consciousness may interpret, or read, its world script, and impulses work their way back from the spiritual world "if we are in a position to receive them."[80] One may well imagine the second Goetheanum in this response and in-streaming impulse: a world Goetheanum. These two buildings, formed out of polarity and in themselves a polarity, visible and invisible, create a foundation for the free spirit's healing work through Anthroposophia.

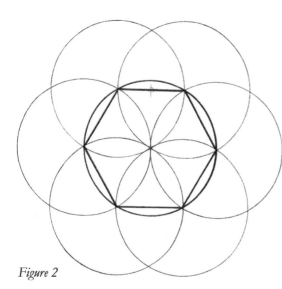

*Figure 1*

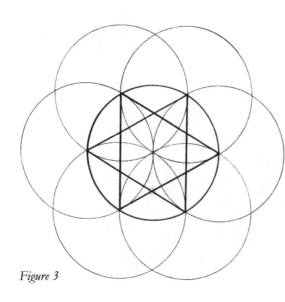

*Figure 2*

*Figure 3*

# Appendix I

There is another way to geometrically construct the relationship of the interpenetrating two cupolas of the first Goetheanum. This second construction method is not tied to its architectural genesis, but it exhibits a geometry that is yet deeply related to the first Goetheanum. This construction method is simple as it is beautiful revealing a hidden number behind the building.

The first Goetheanum may be constructed out of the principle of the number six. Figure 1: The radius of a circle divides the circle's circumference exactly six times. Figure 2: A hexagon is drawn connecting the six points of the circle. Figure 3: A hexagram is drawn connecting the alternate points on the circle. Figure 4: Two circles are drawn, the centers of each on the vertical axis line that intersects hexagon and hexagram. The center of the smaller circle is on the hexagon, and the center of the larger circle is on the hexagram. These two circles have the interpenetrating proportions of the two cupolas of the first Goetheanum.

Hexagon and hexagram forms are created out of the number six, yet with different properties. The hexagon is formed from the radius of the circle, its vertices and sides are the measure of the radius, its close connection to the circle giving it the qualities of wholeness and perfection in space and time. The hexagram's six points interlace two interlocking triangles, its form expressive of the perfect balance of the union of opposites, the marriage of polarities.

If a rhombus (diamond) form's double triangle is drawn through the construction of the two circles (figure 5), their relationship to the two interpenetrating circles reveals a further aspect of the two circles. The large circle circumscribes the lower triangle (point down). The smaller circle partly circumscribes the upper triangle (point up) and partly is inscribed by the triangle (the base line of the triangle).

A circle circumscribing a triangle is an image of the divine enclosing the human soul. A triangle circumscribing a circle is an image of the divine indwelling the human soul. As image, the larger circle expresses the human being enclosed by the divine; the smaller circle shows the soul both within and without the divine, expressive of its earthly and heavenly aspects in the tension of its striving.

Rudolf Steiner used the number principle of six in an early architectural design. Alexander Strakosch gives the account. "The building on Landhauser Strasse 70 in Stuttgart erected in 1911 and dedicated to the anthroposophical work contained in the upper part of the hall window a hexagram (drawing 6). I had expected a pentagram to be placed there and asked Rudolf Steiner, whereupon he answered that the hexagram is the sign for Christ and the far future Venus evolution."[81]

Along the front of the balcony of the lecture room, seals for the seven great evolutionary stages were placed. These seals by Rudolf Steiner were first presented at the Munich Congress. They express the metamorphoses between center and circumference what in the seven capitals express a below and above. The seal is held in a hexagon (drawing 7—Saturn).

Finally, the document that Rudolf Steiner read out loud at the laying of the foundation stone for the first Goetheanum ended with a reference to one planet—and the hour of its appearance—and one zodiacal constellation: "When Mercury as the evening star stood in Libra."[82] (Libra as sign is referred to, not as sidereal constellation.) In the course of one year, the geocentric movement of Mercury forms two interpenetrating triangles in the stations of three superior conjunctions with the sun and three inferior conjunctions with the sun. Mercury has the closest orbit around the sun and has the greatest dependence on the sun—with the sun's path, the great zodiacal circle of the ecliptic. Libra is the smallest constellation in the zodiac, the zodiac's fulcrum with its image of balance. The event of the laying of the foundation stone for the first Goetheanum occurred in the evening when the heavenly body of Mercury shone just above the horizon and just before the autumnal equinox carrying the image of the two interpenetrating triangles in the sign of balance.

This document was placed in the foundation stone for the first Goetheanum composed of two copper dodecahedrons. The dodecahedron relates the number five with the number six in its twelve five sided surfaces. In a conversation with Alexander Strakosch, Rudolf Steiner said, "The dodecahedron, that is the human being."[83]

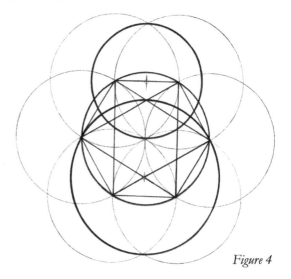

*Figure 4*

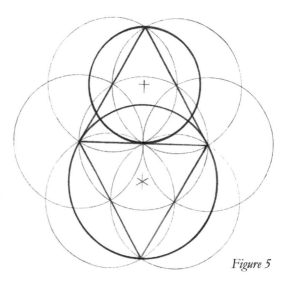

*Figure 5*

*Drawing 6*          *Drawing 7*

# Appendix II

Rudolf Steiner's letters to Marie Steiner in the last weeks of his life ring of his desperate concern for the completion of the building. On 5 March 1925, he writes, "I must be in a fit state to work soon as it does not bear thinking of after everything that has happened if the building had to be interrupted because of my illness." And on 20 March, "The improvement in my health has to be accepted as slow. I hope that I can work on the model of the building in good time so that there is no delay."[84] Rudolf Steiner unexpectedly died ten days later on 30 March 1925. He was unable to carry out the model for the interior of the second Goetheanum.

The present interior design of the building is therefore a compromise born out of necessity. In this regard, the building is still a work in progress. To participate in its building, if even only in thought, is part of the building's heritage. I give the following suggestions as an outcome of this study.

*The Vestibule* and west stairwell with its modern unfinished appearance may yet benefit from color. The vestibule with its three levels is the inner part of the entire west façade, the entrance and exterior sculptural high point of the building. Color in its inner space would help awaken one to its outer intention, expressive of the threefold human being.

A possible color palette is considered. Red for the walls on the vestibule ground level would hold and infuse with strength in a mood of prayer the person who has just entered the building. A viridian middle level would balance a breathing-out dispersing and a breathing-in concentrating in a wakeful mood. A blue third level would give a mantle-like frame of rest to the flame of the Ruby Window. The right value for these colors would need to be found in order to support the space and not dominate it, and a gradation of value from lighter to darker on the wall from ceiling to floor would give it orientation.

*The Use of the Space* in the second Goetheanum that Rudolf Steiner presented on the morning of 31 December 1923 does not in its entirety accord with the present use of the space. The room layout for the building was described as follows. On the ground level, there were to be lecture rooms, studios, practice rooms, the rehearsal stage, and offices. The vestibule space at the terrace level was to be a heated, social area to meet and converse giving access to the rooms on its level. These rooms on the terrace level were to provide spaces for artistic and scientific purposes. A space for the administration of the Anthroposophical Society—the title owner in whose name the building was built—would find its place.

These initial indications may have evolved as the building was realized. However, what had been set forth in the fourteen Statutes during the Christmas Conference was to find realization in the building built in the direction of the manner indicated. Three differentiated ways of working were united: multiplicity in academic pursuits, practice activities, and office spaces on the ground level; artistic and scientific endeavors with social interaction and exchange on the middle level; a unified intent on the third level. The building was to be used to its full capacity for the living fountainhead of anthroposophy.

*The Meeting of Auditorium and Stage* at the curtain remains for me a question how far the union of the two spaces succeeds. Oddly, thirty feet separate the front row of seats from the curtain. An enormous apron stage makes a quasi-second stage creating a no-man's-land when not in use. An abyss yawns between the threshold of stage and auditorium.

The genius of the first Goetheanum was the inter-penetration of the two domes achieved with simple mastery in both interior and exterior of the building. The genius of the second building's exterior's interpenetration of the two halves of the building seems less satisfactorily reflected in its interior. In the second Goetheanum, the interior polar space of square and isosceles trapezoid seem less to interpenetrate and more to abut one another. The apron stage awkwardly attempts this union of the reciprocal spaces. It is by default often improvised for various tasks. Perhaps modified with a trapezoid quality, it could be expanded as a flexible structure accommodating an intimate thrust stage, orchestra pit, podium, and extra seating—a challenge to unite two spaces that freely breathe.

Likewise, the proscenium arch above, adamant and wall-like, awaits a trapezoid-like quality to breathe free.

# Appendix III

*The Plasticine Model* of the building, which Rudolf Steiner created in a few days in the middle of March 1924, is the source for the building plans that were drawn up. However, the building through the vagaries of its history deviates from the model in its outer proportions in many small ways. In order to imagine the building truer, some measures of key differences are listed between the proportions of Rudolf Steiner's model and the present building.

The width: The east length of the building is 13 feet wider than the model. That is, viewed directly east, the stage part, the building is 13 feet too wide. In the north-south axis, the wings are each 5 feet longer than the model. That is, viewed symmetrically directly west or east, the wings extend out 10 feet in total too much. The building is too wide and high in its rear half. A narrower, finer, and smaller east end of the building must be imagined.

The length: the stage part is 3 feet less, and the wings are 3 feet less than the model in the east-west axis. The three-dimensional column is 6 ½ feet too far west compared to the model. A slightly greater accentuation or thrust eastward in the building must be imagined.

The height: The building is 121 feet (37 meters) high at its highest elevation. Its height is constrained to approximate the model. However, no measurement is necessary to perceive the building's greatest error, the lack of differentiation in roofline between the auditorium and stage. The continuum of roofline lets the eye sleep. The differentiation of the stage lower than the auditorium would contrast the two parts of the building and awaken the viewer to the ground plan intention of the building.[85]

*Drawing after the model*

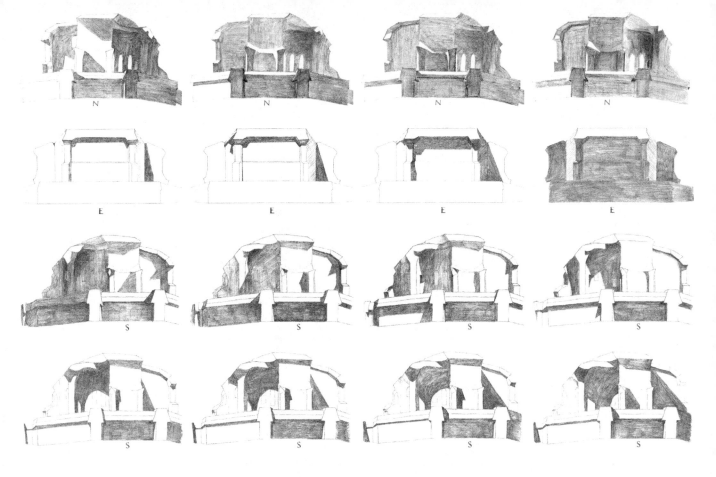

Umbra morphology across the Goetheanum
from sunrise to sunset
at the time of the summer solstice

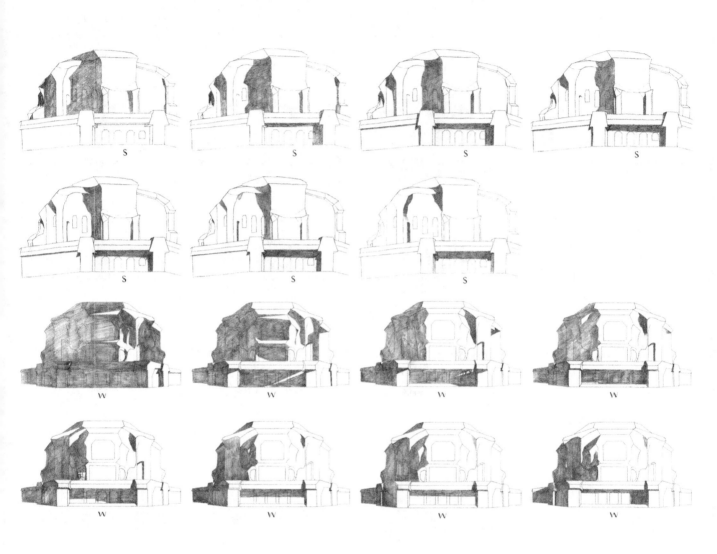

Umbra morphology across the Goetheanum
from sunrise to sunset
at the time of the winter solstice
South: 9:15 — 12:15 and West: 10:30 — 16:00

The weather and the seasons are an intimate and integral part of the building. The Drawing above is a view of the building from the Felsli rondel in spring, in the cherry blossom month of April. The Drawing below depicts the midwinter's midday sun's umbra on the east face of the building. The umbra from the midday sun of midsummer cast on the east face of the building can be compared with it on page 31.

# References and Notes

1. Rudolf Steiner: *CW (Complete Works) 228,* lecture of 14 September 1923.
2. Rudolf Steiner: *CW 79,* lecture of 26 November 1921.
3. *CW 266/2,* lecture of 10 October 1911.
4. *CW 178,* lecture of 15 November 1917.
5. Planting instructions for around the Goetheanum given by Rudolf Steiner to the gardener Antonie Ritter around 1920 as reported in an interview with her daughter Walpurga Nägeli to Esther Gerster in 2009.
6. For Parzival's meeting with Trevrizent in the Ermitage, see Ilona Schubert: *Selbsterlebtes Zusammensein mit Rudolf Steiner und Marie Steiner,* 1977, 2nd ed., 73.
   For Parzival's encounter with the pieta scene of Sigune and Schionatulander near the Ermitage, see Emil Bock: *The Life and Times of Rudolf Steiner,* Vol. 2, 2009 ed., 223.
   For Saint Odile's refuge in the Ermitage, see W. S. Stein: *The Ninth Century and the Holy Grail,* 2001 ed., 290.
7. Erika von Baravalle: *Das Baugestalt des Zweiten Goetheanum als Michaelsbotschaft, Das Goetheanum Wochenschrift,* No. 28, 2006.
8. Boos, Erichsen, and Gut: *Das Goetheanumgelände.*
9. *CW 284,* lecture of 21 May 1907.
10. *CW 349,* lecture of 21 February 1923.
11. *Mitteilungen,* IV, 1997, No. 202.
12. *Stilformen des Organisch-Lebendigen:* Rudolf Steiner: lecture of 30 December 1921.
13. John James: *Chartres,* 96.
14. *CW 271,* lecture of 15 February 1918.
15. *CW 115,* lecture of 26 October 1909.
16. *CW 201,* lectures 9 and 11 April 1920.
17. *CW 286,* lecture of 23 January 1914.
18. Ibid.
19. *CW 286,* lecture of 17 June 1914.
20. *CW 275,* lecture of 29 December 1914.
21. *CW 204,* lecture of 23 April 1921.
22. *CW 201,* lecture of 9 April 1920.
23. Ibid.
24. *CW 205,* lecture of 2 July 1921.
25. *CW 236,* lecture of 27 April 1924.

26. Henri Bortoft: *The Wholeness of Nature.*

27. Owen Barfield: *What Coleridge Thought,* chapter 3.

28. *CW 108,* lecture of 13 November 1908.

29. *CW 129,* lecture of 23 August 1911.

30. See note 26 above.

31. Ibid.

32. *CW 4,* 1964 edition, 28, 86, 89.

33. *CW 181,* lecture of 3 July 1918.

34. Lecture of 16 October 1920.

35. *CW 282,* lecture of 7 September 1924.

36. *CW 223,* lecture of 2 April 1923.

37. *CW 254,* lecture of 24 October 1915.

38. Alexander Strakosch: *Lebenswege mit Rudolf Steiner.*

39. *CW 286,* lecture of 17 June 1914.

40. *CW 286,* lecture of 28 June 1914.

41. Andrew Beard (ed.): *Rudolf Steiner Architecture,* 115–116.

42. *CW 275,* lecture of 28 December 1914.

43. See note 35 above.

44. *CW 158,* lecture of 21 November 1914.

45. *CW 286,* lecture of 12 December 1911.

46. *CW 293,* lecture of 26 August 1919.

47. *CW 233a,* lecture of 12 January 1924.

48. *CW 101* (German edition), lecture of 28 December 1907.

49. See note 35 above.

50. *CW 284/285,* lecture of 15 October 1911.

51. Rudolf Steiner: *Die Goetheanum Fenster.*

52. Ibid.

53. Ibid.

54. *CW 106,* 10 September 1908.

55. *CW 289/290,* lecture of 25 August 1921.

56. *CW 95,* lecture of 24 August 1906.

57. *CW 95,* lecture of 26 August 1906.

58. *CW 284,* October 1907:
    *Pictures of the Apocalyptic Seals and Columns:*
    *An Introduction to the Portfolio of Fourteen Plates.*

59. Karl Stockmeyer: *The Model Building of Malsch.*

60. Eric Zimmer: *Der Modellbau von Malsch,* 16.

61. *CW 93a,* lecture of 7 October 1905.

62. *CW 93,* lecture of 22 May 1905.

63. *CW 204,* lecture of 23 April 1921.

64. *CW 93,* lecture of 22 May 1905.

65. See note 60 above.

66. Rudolf Grosse: *The Christmas Foundation.*

67. Assya Turgeniev: *Reminiscences of Rudolf Steiner and Work on the First Goetheanum.*

68. Daniel Bemmelen: *Rudolf Steiner's New Approach to Color on the Ceiling of the First Goetheanum.*

69. Reese Palley: *Concrete, A Seven-Thousand-Year History.*

70. See note 34 above.

71. *CW 156,* lecture of 7 October 1914.

72. Carl Kemper: *Der Bau.*

73. *CW 260,* 72.

74. Ibid., See manuscripts at the end of the book.

75. Ibid., 73.

76. Ibid., Principle 4 of the Anthroposophical Society.

77. Admission's brochure for the Anthroposophical Society in America.

78. *CW 200,* lecture of 17 October 1920.

79. *CW 270-III,* 190.

80. *CW 233a,* lecture of 22 April 1924.

81. *STIL* 1983/84, V. Heft 4, Alexander Strakosch.

82. See note 66 above.

83. See note 81 above.

84. *CW 262,* 255 and 260.

85. Measurements sourced from *Eloquent Concrete* by Raab, Klingborg, and Fant; a study from the Arts Section; plans from the Plans Archive; and from *Anthroposophy World Wide,* Nr. 6/13.

## *Credits for the Original Drawings sketched in this Book*

Page 9. Plans Archive.

Pages 30 and 31 (below). *Mitteilungen,* IV, 1997, No. 202.

Page 42 (above). *Das Goetheanum Wochenschrift,* No. 40, 2008.

Page 43 (middle). Raab, Klingborg, and Fant: *Eloquent Concrete.*

Page 68 (above). Werner Blaser: *Nature in Buildings.*

Page 68 (middle). *Das Wirken Rudolf Steiners,* Band IV, 267.

Page 84. Goetheanum Archive.

Page 108. *STIL,* 04/1979, Albert von Baravalle.

Page 114. Hilde Raske: *Language of Color in the First Goetheanum.*

Page 131 (below). John Fletcher: *Art Inspired by Rudolf Steiner.*

Made in the USA
Middletown, DE
17 October 2023

40946427R00084